FALMOUTH HAVEN

The Maritime History of a Great West Country Port

FALMOUTH HAVEN

The Maritime History of a Great West Country Port

D.G. WILSON

The History Press

BIOGRAPHICAL NOTE

David Wilson has had many years of experience in amateur archaeology, local history studies and sailing traditional craft. He has previously published books on the history of the Thames, including *The Thames, Record of a Working Waterway*, and *The Victorian Thames*. Following a career as a Thames lockkeeper he retired to Cornwall ten years ago and has since produced the booklet *The Mills of a Cornish Valley*. He sails on the Fal regularly, is a member of the Cornwall Wildlife Trust, the Cornish Maritime Trust, and a volunteer at the National Maritime Museum, Cornwall.

Back cover: Falmouth working-boat, *Stella*.

First published in 2007 by Tempus Publishing

Reprinted in 2008 by
The History Press
The Mill, Brimscombe Port,
Stroud, Gloucestershire, GL5 2QG
www.thehistorypress.co.uk

Reprinted 2009

British Library Cataloguing in Publication Data.
A catalogue record for this book is available from the British Library.

ISBN 978 0 7524 4226 6

Typesetting and origination by
Tempus Publishing Limited.
Printed and bound in England.

CONTENTS

ACKNOWLEDGEMENTS

My thanks to the following for their courtesy and assistance as I explored many avenues of research. The staff of The Cornwall Centre, Redruth; The Cornwall County Record Office, Truro; The Royal Institution of Cornwall, Truro; The Falmouth Art Gallery; The National Maritime Museum, Greenwich; members of the Royal Cornwall Polytechnic Society, Falmouth, particularly Peter Gilson and Michael Bradley; volunteer staff of the Bartlett Library, National Maritime Museum, Cornwall; Dennis Bennett, Michael Goodchild, Dougie Graham, Brian Jose, John Mitchell, June Palmer, Tony Pawlyn, Alan Pearson, Mary Rich, Roger Stephens, Jo Warburton, and Ian Wilson. Special thanks to my wife Roma for computer work and transferring my longhand scrawl to disc.

Sources of illustrations are given at the end of captions. All other photographs are by the author.

PROLOGUE

Among the earliest recollections of my childhood were visits to a place I thought very delightful, because it combined the special charms of sea and country. In those days I lived in a Midland city, in a large house at the end of a terrace, where the rooms were spacious and the garden small, and which looked out upon a public road and the gravelled walk leading to a pump-room. Hence when my parents, led by old associations and familiar ties, took 'the children' to Falmouth, we enjoyed the rare freedom of frocks bedabbled with sea-water, and little hands, embrowned by the sun, which escaped being gloved. Well do I remember the yellow shells – real treasures – picked up on the beaches at the Bar, which no longer exists, and the delightful pools left by the receding tide! And then the strolls up the 'rope-walk', a tree-shadowed lane where wild flowers grew in the hedges, and which emerged by a curve into a winding road above, where more wild flowers were to be found, and not the ghost of a house was to be seen except Gylling Dune....

Susan Elizabeth Gay, *Old Falmouth*, 1903

INTRODUCTION

Formed in remote times by cataclysmic natural forces, the Falmouth Estuary evolved into one of the largest and most beautiful harbours in the world. For hundreds of years its deep-water channels and quiet creeks, sheltered by tree-clad shores, have provided mariners with protection from storm and enemy alike. Over the centuries ships manned by crews from many countries have graced the waters of the Fal, emphasising its importance in international maritime affairs. Within the haven, ships were built: sailing ships to carry Cornish products to far-away harbours, to return with raw materials and luxuries otherwise unobtainable. Smaller craft of many kinds were needed, such as luggers, smacks and punts, for fishing, carrying, ferrying and for leisure. The need for such craft increased in parallel with the growth of the shore-side communities such as Truro, Penryn and Falmouth. Many small shipyards were established, especially around the latter town developing near the harbour entrance. The population also had to eat, bread was a staple of life: apart from watermills on many watershed streams, the tide was also harnessed to grind corn into flour. One of the favoured locations for these vital industries was the Bar, part of the foreshore close to Arwenack House, the home of the Killigrews, founders of Falmouth. The old shipyards and tide mills have now gone, vanished beneath modern development. This work is an attempt to bring them back to life, and place the Bar in its rightful place within the broader history of a great West Country port.

ONE

The Foundation of Falmouth

A ROCKY SHORE

One of the most notable views in Cornwall is to be had from the headland of Pendennis, the great rock promontory which guards and shelters the ancient harbour of Falmouth: even more spectacular is the higher view from St Anthony Head, its opposite partner on the far side of the harbour entrance. From here the cliffs of Cornwall stretch eastwards towards the awesome bulk of Dodman Point, 18km away: and beyond, on a good day, can be seen the coast of South Devon. Westwards, beyond Pendennis Castle and at the entrance to Penryn River, lies Falmouth town and its busy docks. Sweeping towards the south, the protective curve of Falmouth Bay takes the eye towards the ship-breaking Manacle Rocks, on the easterly point of the Lizard Peninsula. There is further spectacle to the north: beyond St Mawes Castle lies the Fal Estuary, otherwise known as Carrick Roads, the third largest natural harbour in the world. Above and beyond its tree-clad shores can be seen the granite uplands of the interior of Cornwall. The estuary can be likened to the palm of a slender hand, its fingers being numerous creeks in deep valleys extending for miles towards the hills.

Valleys are, in the main, created by running water: however, in Cornwall there are now only tiny streams running through ravines which have been cut deeply into the ancient rocks of slate and sandstone. As for the Fal Estuary itself, faults caused by earth movements in the underlying rocks may have helped the sea to open it up, nevertheless, it is known that for tens of thousands of years the sea was nowhere near. In simple terms, the reason for such a vast amount of erosion concerns the Ice Age, or a number of ice ages, which began about one-and-a-half-million years ago, when the land surface of the South West, with hills much higher than today, sloped gently southwards for tens of kilometres further than at present before it reached the sea. Britain was part of Europe, and even Scilly to the west was a much larger land mass than today, and at times also joined to Cornwall. There have been four or more glacial periods, varying in length and severity, within the overall Ice Age, with the longest estimated as lasting about 100,000 years. The glacials were

A panoramic view from the hill above Penryn, looking southwards along the Penryn River. Falmouth town and Pendennis are on the right and Flushing to the left. Opposite Pendennis are the headlands of St Mawes and St Anthony. Carrick Roadstead is off to the left. (John Maggs, Antiquarian Prints.)

interspersed by warmer temperate, or even semi-tropical periods, one of which might be approaching now! In the cold periods, ice sheets, in places to a depth of hundreds of metres, advanced from the north across Britain. Glaciers reached as far as the Thames Valley, and one sheet, it is thought, to Scilly. The land surface of Cornwall would have been frozen to great depths below an arctic landscape. Over thousands of years of winter freezing and summer thaw, rivers carried frost-shattered surface rock debris towards the distant sea, carving their way along ancient fault lines in the underlying geology. The scale of the erosion may be imagined by multiplying a Lynmouth or Boscastle catastrophe by any number of times and having it last for thousands of years.

So much water was held in polar regions during glacial periods that sea levels have been estimated at being up to 120m below those at present, allowing river systems such as the Fal to carve deep gorges into the landscape. The Fal River would have roared past the Pendennis promontory towards a distant sea through a deep channel, which has been identified offshore well below the present seabed. When polar ice began to melt during the warmer interglacials, sea levels rose to heights well above those of today, forming the raised beaches which exist around our coasts. The sea also drowned the previous Ice Age river channels and their deep valleys, thereby creating estuaries such as the Fal. These drowned valleys are more properly known as *rias*. The last ice age began to rapidly recede a mere 15,000 years ago; as world temperatures increased, the tundra landscape which existed around our coasts was steadily colonised by temperate forest. From Pendennis the Fal River may have appeared as a rushing stream at the bottom of a lush tree-clad gorge. Further out, parts of the coastal plain forest would have been explored and perhaps settled by Bronze Age peoples, who, over generations, found that they had to re-establish

Evening sky over Pendennis, looking west. The pilot boat is returning to port.

their settlements further inland as the sea returned. Although such sites have not been identified yet under the sea off mainland coasts, hut foundations and field walls litter the scabed between some of the Isles of Scilly, which as late as Roman times was practically one large island.

As the sea flooded the Fal again the valley was filled with sands and silts, covering the coastal forests. Remnants of this vegetation have been found at many places in recent times, particularly during low spring tides. These sites include Mounts Bay, Hayle, Porthleven, Helford, Fowey, and several locations on the Fal. In Victorian times, when discovered accidentally during local harbour works, water-logged branches and tree trunks were great curiosities, and posed perplexing questions as to their origin. At the annual meeting of the Royal Institution of Cornwall in November 1871, it was reported that during excavations for foundations of the new pier at Market Strand in Falmouth, remains of a submarine forest were discovered. The layer, extending for about 2m below low water spring tides, consisted of compacted peat with flags (reeds?) and ferns, and included tree trunks up to 30cm in diameter. Species identified included hazel, oak, fir, beech and birch. The layer was said to extend for some distance up into the area called the Moor. More pertinent to this narrative, traces of a similar forest were discovered at the Bar pools. From theories expressed at the time it is obvious that the concept of sea level rise was not then appreciated.

Further inland, some ancient remains of human activity were discovered during nineteenth-century alluvial tin mining operations in Restronguet Creek, one of the Fal 'fingers', which had filled up over thousands of years with muds and silts washed from the hills. Deep below the present creek bed were discovered plant remains and traces of Bronze Age mining activities in the form of antler picks and a bronze axe, proving that 4,000 years ago people were already exploiting the mineral wealth of Cornwall. The great rock of Pendennis stood proud of the many changes to the landscape surrounding it, and in common with many other cliff-top promontories on the Cornish coast is believed to have been defended with earthworks in the Iron Age, its banks and ditches obliterated by the building of the Tudor castle. A more unobtrusively sited fort, believed to be Iron Age,

The lighthouse on St Anthony Head, since 1835 guiding mariners past the craggy approaches to Falmouth Haven. Pendennis to the left is 2km away. Easterly winds are expected and sailing ships lie safely at anchor in the lee of St Anthony, *c.*1900. (RCPS.)

lies in a strategic defensive position at Roundwood on the Upper Fal. Many other Iron Age and Romano-British sites are scattered throughout the region, including at the new university campus overlooking the Penryn River, where excavations have revealed finds dating from the Mesolithic. For thousands of years people from these communities have used the Fal for hunting, fishing and navigation.

Until the late twentieth century, which saw the enlargement of Falmouth Docks, the development of Port Pendennis marina village and the National Maritime Museum, Cornwall, the southern end of the Falmouth waterfront was known as the Bar. The name is perpetuated in Bar Road, which skirts what was once the southern edge of a large area of sand banks and tidal pools now all covered in consolidated rubble, concrete and steel piling with, it has to be said, some rather interesting buildings placed on top. The term 'bar', aquatically speaking, is usually descriptive of areas of sand, shingle, or pebbles, sometimes exposed at low tides, thrown up into a bank by the action of waves or tidal currents. Navigationally, bars have caused the deaths of countless mariners, or at least given an uncomfortable passage in passing them. The bar at the entrance to Salcombe Harbour is a case in point, and the Doom Bar, below Padstow on the Camel Estuary, needs no further comment. The Fal and Penryn Rivers also have bars which have been marked on charts from early times. In 1597 Baptista Boazio published a detailed chart of the Fal, identifying several, including a 'Barre' near Penryn; at 'Turner Weer Point',

Pendennis Castle and Falmouth Harbour, *c.*1960. The outer bulwarks are shrouded by trees in summer growth. The photograph illustrates the extent of the wharves and drydocks which are busy with shipping. (RCPS.)

towards Trelissick; and the prominent 'Barre of Pencro', now known as Mylor or North Bank. There was another 'Barre' on the north side of the Pendennis peninsular, a location which in later years became 'Bar Point', and which in 1861 was cut away to make room for the new docks.

The development of the docks considerably altered the ancient course of tidal streams flowing to and fro along the Penryn River and Falmouth waterfront. Previously, the currents sweeping past the sheltered bay between Bar Point and the waterfront would have caused eddies, which over the centuries deposited material to form a great curving bank, covered only perhaps at the highest tides, encompassing one, or perhaps two, tidal pools. This area became known as Arwenack Bar. The shore side of the Bar is located in an area of low-lying ground at the base of a combe or small valley in the centre of which sits Falmouth town railway station. Deposition of silt from this valley in remote times may also have contributed to the formation of the Bar. A small stream from a spring-head still flows down the valley, and is shown on early Ordnance Survey maps flowing into the shallows of the Bar, contributing on its way to a large tidal timber pond which existed where in 2005 there is now a new car park. Most of the stream is obviously now piped underground. It is said that contractors building the new marina village in the late 1980s were unaware of its presence, until it burst through their new foundations. Drastic measures had to be taken to divert it through pipes into the harbour.

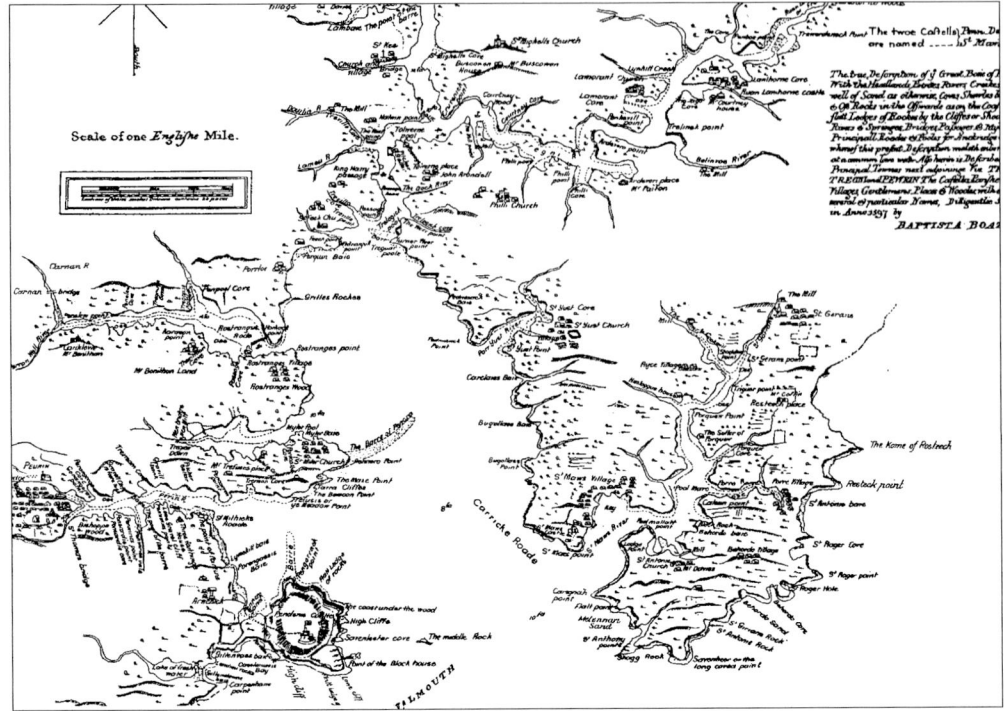

'The True Description of the Great Baie of Falmouth' by Baptista Boazio, 1597. (Cornwall Centre.)

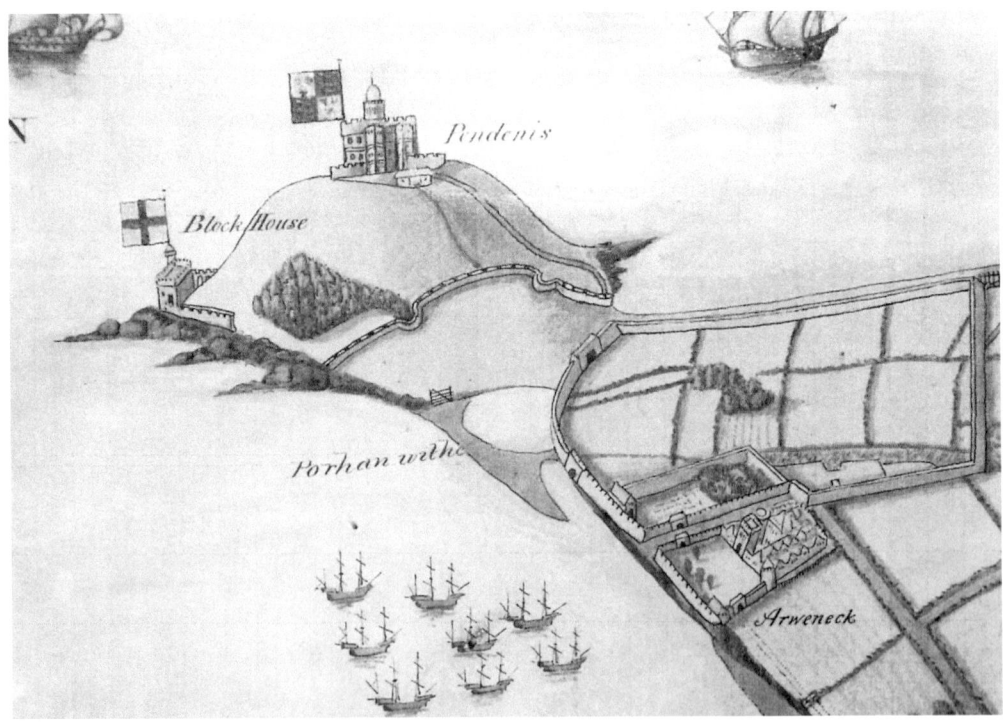

Detail of Pendennis and Arweneck, from the Elizabethan 'Burghley' map. (RCPS.)

ARWENACK AND THE KILLIGREWS

Early maps and charts of the Fal environs depict our particular bar area in different ways, depending on the skill of the cartographer and how important the area was thought to be. Interpretation can be a little difficult: however, a general pattern of the evolution of the landscape, and seascape, emerges. In 1597 Boazio calls areas of Falmouth waterfront 'Lymekill (kiln?) Baie', and 'Porengassis Baie'; his 'Barre' off Pendennis has already been noted. The Bar area seems to be shown as a sandbank, but the name he gives it is difficult to interpret, possibly being 'Penrem', 'Penero', or 'Porrem Sand'.

Dating roughly to the same period, or a decade or so earlier, the 'Burghley' map, a copy of which was found among the Killigrew Estate records, came originally from a collection of papers of William Cecil, Lord Burghley, Queen Elizabeth's Lord Treasurer. The map *may* have been commissioned during a review of the Fal Harbour defences. Perhaps even Sir Walter Raleigh had a hand in it on one of his visits, conferring with Sir John Killigrew, Governor of Pendennis Castle, at the latter's mansion at nearby Arwenack. The map shows the manor house in detail, with a wall or palisade enclosing parkland across the isthmus to the Gyllyngvase shore of Falmouth Bay. A barred gate on the end of the curving sand bar may denote a route from Arwenack to the castle: a 'Walkers Gate' is mentioned in a mid-eighteenth century estate lease, delineating the bounds of the Bar property. The name 'Porhan Withe' seems to be applied to the Bar, but it is not known by that name on other documents. *Porhan*, pronounced 'Poran', was the ancient title applied to the hillside directly behind Custom House Quay. There existed a Porhan Street until the 1960s when it was incorporated into New Street. A single large natural pool is depicted within the sandbar, which appears to be continuous from shore to shore. Presumably, if this was the case, there would have been an exchange of sea water within the pool at high tides. The area must have been very beautiful then: human habitation consisted of little more than Pendennis Castle, Arwenack and cottages of fisherfolk at Smithick, alias Pennycomequick, a small hamlet in the vicinity of what became Market Strand and the Prince of Wales Pier. Hanging woods covered the hillsides, and fish and bird life abounded in the Bar pool. One can perhaps compare the imaginary scene with one of the tranquil reaches of the Upper Fal today.

The ancient Cornish family of Killigrew is said to have acquired the lands of Arwenack from Walter Bronescombe, the Bishop of Exeter, in about 1264, a nearby house at Kergilliack, in Budock, being a seat of the bishops. The Church owned extensive property in the area, including around Penryn, where, at about the same date, Bronescombe founded Glasney College at the tidal head of Penryn Creek. It became a famous centre of religious education. From being a small fishing community, the town of Penryn grew up around the college, with a harbour and quays accessible at high tides. Apparently the inhabitants were involved in various illicit activities, including smuggling and piracy, which seem to have been commonplace along the coasts from early times. In spite of its lawlessness Penryn received a Royal Charter in 1621 and continued a maritime trade into the twentieth century.

For perhaps several thousand years the whole area of the Falmouth Estuary had been known to sea traders, settlers, pirates, and invading fleet commanders by various Celtic,

Penryn 1816. Vessels lie alongside the seventeenth-century Exchequer Quay. Cargoes were handled here and at the other quays on the two tidal creeks into the twentieth century. (RCPS.)

Cornish, or Saxon equivalents of the name Fal-mouth. In mid-fifteenth-century Chancery Court proceedings Falmouth is named on a number of occasions as the place of origin of pirate ships. As there was no town of that name, the crews would have anchored their craft in sheltering creeks of the Fal, and perhaps used Truro and Penryn for occasional accommodation and provisioning. Fowey, a much busier port at the time, would have been their main base. Two of the more notorious pirates were Nicholas Frychowe and Hankyn Seelander, who used both Fowey and Falmouth from which to maraud up and down the English Channel, pillaging French, Flemish, Breton and Spanish ships with impunity. As with the smuggling trade in later centuries, officials were quite happy to receive a bribe of stolen wine to ignore petitions of complaint from foreign merchants. Seelander is recorded as sailing with small squadrons of vessels, variously drawn from Falmouth, Truro, Fowey and Plymouth. Frychowe did likewise, one of his Falmouth-based ships having the beautiful name of *La Fleur de la Mer*: indubitably captured from the French. Other vessels mentioned were a 'great ship of Falmouth', barges and balingers. The latter type is thought to have been a two-masted, square-rigged ship, commonly of between 25 and 60 tons. Large crews are recorded, inferring that oars could be used, enabling a pirate ship to close with any slow merchantman in light winds. Records show that the greatest number of English balingers traded (or raided) out of Devon and Cornish ports. In 1548, long before there was a town of this name, commissioners of Edward VI reported on '...the fayer havyn named Falmouth to which sometimes resort one hundred great shippes...' The town of Truro, 14km from the mouth of the estuary, traditionally held jurisdiction, including collecting harbour and custom dues, over the whole estuary apart from the Bishops of Exeter's Penryn River. From at least the sixteenth century another title, Carrig or Carrick Roads, came into common parlance for the main 6km-long deep-water anchorage.

In about 1385 the Killigrew family moved into a stone-built manor house beside the Bar pool at Arwenack: a location which was sheltered from Channel storms but not

High tide on the Penryn River, *c.*1910. Barge *Rose* of Falmouth is alongside the ancient granite-built quay on St Gluvias Creek. The site is now occupied by a bizarre modern development, inappropriate to Penryn's maritime past. (Bartlett Library, NMMC.)

Old fishing boats at Exchequer Quay, Penryn, 2006. To the right business premises and boatyards line the road to Ponsharden and Falmouth.

exactly safe from marauding pirates, slave traders, or enemy ships of war. However, by the sixteenth century the house boasted a defensive palisade and became even better protected when, in the 1540s, King Henry VIII had the forts of St Mawes and Pendennis constructed to control the harbour entrance. Now it was possible for deep-draughted trading vessels to anchor with relative safety within the roadstead, and what became known as the Inner Harbour within the Bar Point sand bar and close to Arwenack. Henry appointed John Killigrew as first Governor of Pendennis Castle, and as a privilege of the office the King granted him the customary dues of both Penryn and Truro Harbour, much to the chagrin of both towns. However, these rights were later restored to them when the bounds of the separate harbour for Falmouth town were established.

Only a few particulars of the confusing history of the Killigrew family can be included here. Some held high positions as Governors of Pendennis, Members of Parliament and royal courtiers. But their lives reflected the turbulent Elizabethan and Stuart periods, and their outer respectability could sometimes hold dark secrets. Life could be short, you made the best you could of it, especially if it meant breaking laws that couldn't be enforced anyway. Death could come from starvation, disease, or, on the western shores, at the hands of marauding North African slave traders or Dunkirk privateers. A vast number of the population, especially the local gentry, supplemented their income from smuggling. Goods brought in by various means included luxuries such as Oriental silks, lace, gin and brandy, and basics such as otherwise taxable salt for pilchard processing. Following the example of Sir Walter Raleigh, who probably visited Arwenack, some of the Killigrew sons obtained official Letters of Marque, commanding privateers to pillage enemy merchant ships in time of war, a common practice on all sides. A local act of piracy occurred in the winter of 1582, and involved Dame Mary Killigrew, wife of John Killigrew the Second. A brief outline of the story is that because of adverse winds, a Spanish merchant ship had come into the haven and anchored close to Arwenack (a situation which compares to a Catholic fly being within a hair's breadth of an Elizabethan spider's web). At night, while the merchants from the ship were resting at an inn in Penryn, the crew were overpowered by unknown men and thrown overboard, but not killed. Apparently, Dame Killigrew knew about, or had instigated the piracy, and sent two of her retainers to obtain her share of the cargo before the ship was smuggled away to Ireland. They returned with their plunder to Arwenack, and it was divided amongst the women in the household and friends in Penryn, Dame Mary being displeased with her meagre share of Hollands cloth and leather, which was put in a cask and buried in the garden. As the commissioners at the later enquiry consisted of Sir John Killigrew and other local gentry, nothing came of the matter.

It is said that some of the 'more respectable pirates' actually stayed with the Killigrews at Arwenack, their ships no doubt openly laying at anchor off the Bar. If Royal Navy ships were expected in the area, they may have moved across Falmouth Bay to Helford. The Helford Estuary, bordering the Killigrew Estates to the west, was regularly used as a haven for pirates for much of the Elizabethan age. Several creeks and bays provided safe anchorage from rough weather out at sea, and its narrow entrance and difficult navigation, plus a likely hostile reception, were deterrents to vessels searching for them. Illicit cargoes could be unloaded at hidden quays and spirited away into the countryside with the full

Pendennis Castle in the eighteenth century. A typical 'semi-aerial' view of the time, by which the main features could be illustrated. King Henry VIII's circular artillery fort was surrounded at later dates by formidable ramparts and bastions by using the natural slopes of the headland. (Cornwall Centre.)

St Mawes Castle at the mouth of the Percuil River, 2006.

co-operation of the Killigrews, who could provide horses and armed escorts if necessary. Wealthy friends and kinsmen in the area were the willing recipients of wine and luxury goods, the Killigrews naturally receiving goods or a cut of the profits.

Sir John Killigrew the Third, while Governor of Pendennis during the time of the threatened Spanish Armada, was suspected of planning to assist the invaders if they attempted to make a bridgehead in Cornwall. For this, debt, and other misdemeanours, he spent years in prison, where he died in 1605. His young son, the fourth Sir John, had the misfortune to be married off, in the vain hope of a large dowry to restore the family fortunes, to Jane, daughter of Sir George Fermor. Some writers have confused Jane with the earlier Mary Killigrew and her act of piracy against the Spanish ship. Instead, Jane became notorious for another reason, this being her affair with Sir Nicholas Parker, who was Governor of Pendennis in the years up to 1614, and for which her husband petitioned for a divorce. It may have been at this time that Jane fled to Penryn. Allegedly in 'great misery', she was received by the Mayor and Corporation and given accommodation. Penryn, never seeing eye to eye with the Killigrews and their fledgling new settlement, must have rejoiced at this coup. It took Sir John ten years to arrange a divorce, taking any money he had left. He died in about 1633, like his father, in debt.

Possibly because of the divorce settlement, it seems that Lady Jane was allowed to stay at Arwenack, and in control of the manor estates, marrying a Captain Francis Bluett, of nearby Trevethan. The couple were not allowed to have many years of wedded bliss, for the bloody conflict of the Civil War was spreading into Cornwall. In 1646 Pendennis was besieged by parliamentary forces, the Governor of the castle at that time being eighty-

Opposite: Gweek, at the head of the beautiful Helford River, *c.*1900. Once the haunt of smugglers and pirates and ships loading Cornish tin. The schooner, drying sails on a windless day, is moored at Lower Quay. Riverside House, built in 1891, was demolished in recent years to make way for a large industrial building. (Royal Institution of Cornwall.)

Right: This notice published in the *Royal Cornwall Gazette* demonstrates that the Helford River, bordering the parish of Constantine, was still being used as a smuggling route. The trade elsewhere was on the decline, and the large reward shows that the authorities were making considerable efforts to stamp it out. This account of a vicious attack must scotch any romanticised view of smugglers.

CUSTOM HOUSE, LONDON,
26th November, 1828.

WHEREAS it has been represented to the Commissioners of His Majesty's Customs, that in the Night of the 19th November, instant, a large party of Men (armed with Pistols, Bludgeons, and Knives,) in the act of conveying Smuggled Goods from the Coast, were intercepted by two Officers of the Customs near CONSTANTINE CHURCH TOWN, in the Parish of CONSTANTINE, in the *County of Cornwall :* and that the said Officers seized from the said Persons several Horses laden with Spirits, which had been run on shore without payment of Duties : and that after the said Officers had so seized the Horses and Goods, the Smugglers with force and violence rescued the same from them, at the same time feloniously assaulting and ill-treating the said Officers, so that the life of one of them is despaired of.

The said Commissioners are hereby pleased to offer

A REWARD OF £300

to any person or persons, who shall discover or cause to be discovered any one or more of the persons concerned in the said Outrage, so that he or they may be apprehended and dealt with according to Law, to be paid by the Collector of His Majesty's Customs at the *PORT OF FALMOUTH,* in the said County of Cornwall, upon Conviction.

By Order of the Commissioners,
T. WHITMORE, Secretary.

year-old Colonel John Arundel of Trerice. The district suffered terribly from the foraging of large numbers of troops, entrenchments were thrown up around the castle by both defenders and attackers, and unfortunately for Jane and Bluett, Arwenack House was burnt. After five months Arundel capitulated, Pendennis being the last of King Charles' strongholds in England to do so, and the starving garrison was allowed to march out with full honours. On the death of Lady Jane in 1648, Peter, the next eldest brother to the fourth Sir John, succeeded to the Killigrew title and his depleted inheritance at Arwenack. He had had many contacts at the Court of King Charles I, where he was known as 'a fine gentleman' and later rumoured to have helped Charles in his abortive attempt to escape to the Continent in November 1647. However, he seems to have had no problems in taking up his inheritance under Cromwell's government and he moved to Cornwall to take control of the estates. In 1660 he was given Governorship of Pendennis and the following year knighted by the newly crowned Charles II.

THE EARLY PORT

In the first decade of the seventeenth century the custom house at Truro was recording imports of coal from South Wales; timber and barrel staves from Ireland; iron, lead, glass and nails from Bristol; timber, bricks and stone from Middleburg, Netherlands; and salt, pitch, wines, vinegar, raisins, figs and prunes from Bordeaux and La Rochelle. Penryn was recording similar imports including 'elephants teeth' (ivory) from Flushing in the

Arwenack manor house in 1786. Following the siege of Pendennis much of the fabric remained ruinous. It was later renovated to a different plan but today retains its ancient appearance. (Cornwall Centre.)

Truro in 1816. The tidal waters of the River Kenwyn (left) form a wide basin flanked by Back and Lemon Quays. The River Allen to the right skirts St Mary's Church, site of the later cathedral. Boscawen Bridge was to span this inlet, speeding the process of infilling of the creeks. To the left the artist has depicted the arrival of a cutter, schooner and lugger. (Cornwall Centre.)

Netherlands. The *Larke* of London arrived with a cargo of iron, lead, timber, pitch, tar, potash, brown paper, ironmongery, chests of glasses, groceries, haberdashery and household stuff. Pilchards were already being exported to La Rochelle and Naples. Vessels involved in the London and Continental voyages included the *Maudlyn* and *John* of Falmouth, therefore the name of the port was already becoming known internationally.

The haven, having numerous coves and beaches for vessels to 'take the ground', was frequently used for refitting and hull re-caulking and cleaning, known as 'graving'. In 1634 King Charles' Admiral of the Narrow Seas, Sir John Pennington, recommended to the Admiralty that to improve sailing qualities Royal Navy ships were graved as frequently as other nations, particularly the Dutch, who beached their ships every two or three months for this. He particularly recommended Falmouth for this, partly because '… there the Hollanders do ordinarily ground their ships and wash and tallow and presently off again. I have seen a dozen at a time do it, and until your Lordships take this course we shall be able to do little good with our ships, either for the taking of pirates or others…'

From early in the century the Killigrews had encouraged settlement on the land around Smithick, a few hundred metres along the shore from their manor house, and in 1613 had received a favourable response from King James I for the establishment of a town. It was granted a custom house in 1650 and a market in 1652, with a mayor and town council, and in 1664 became a separate parish from Budock and Gluvias. The settlement already had a sizeable population, estimated by Whetter at about 700, this figure possibly doubling by 1688, numbers often swelled by mariners and travellers in transit. All required a focal point to provide for their spiritual needs and therefore Peter Killigrew gave land for the construction of a parish church. This was completed by 1664, and dedicated to King Charles the Martyr, as a tribute to the father of Charles II. Following a Charter of Incorporation in 1661, another Act of 1665, or 1670, confirmed the boundaries of the new borough, which was to be called Falmouth 'after the name of the harbour'. In 1671 a new Act granted Peter Killigrew the Second the authority to build a 'Charles' or 'New' quay (Custom House/Town Quay) and make charges for ships using it. Construction work soon began: within two years the Arwenack Estate was making payments for timber, deals, and gravel at the quay and cellars, for workmen and labourers at the pier, and Eastman for the use of his barges carrying stones. The quay was for 'securing the shipping from the easterly winds which do sometimes annoy and endanger them', a sentiment with which all present-day local mariners can empathise. This Act, and another of 1676, confirmed the estuary harbour rights of Truro north of the boundary between Mylor Bank and St Just Creek, and also confirmed the ancient rights of the Bishops of Exeter on the Penryn River, although for years Sir Francis Godolphin claimed he was lessee, and eventually accused of extorting various dues from ships in the harbour to which he was not entitled. These are the bare essentials of considerable legislation concerning the establishment of Falmouth and its harbour.

The town grew rapidly as dwellings, shops, boatyards, lodging houses and a number of inns proliferated along the waterfront. A contemporary visitor remarked on the town's growth, stating it 'is now become a great place… it consists chiefly of ale houses'. The town became busy supplying goods and services to the castle garrison and visiting ships; there was a regular post service by road to London, and also by sea via Plymouth. In

Falmouth town in 1827, by Richard Thomas. All the surrounding farmland would disappear under new streets and housing in the next century or so. Market Strand, in the centre of the waterfront, is the site of the original fishing settlement of Smithick. The harbour low-water depths are given in feet. (Cornwall Centre.)

From the harbour the parish church tower stands out boldly above the town roofs. Fishing boats rest on the outer wall of the town quay at low tide.

about 1688 there began the famous Falmouth packet service to Spain, expanding later to Portugal, the Mediterranean, Caribbean, and North and South America. From the second half of the century tradesmen and merchants began to settle in the town, hoping to take advantage of the commercial possibilities envisaged by the Killigrews. With the export of various cargoes such as fish from Penryn and tin from Truro, these towns didn't entirely lose their trade to the upstart settlement, but soon Falmouth was to have more vessels, and of larger size, belonging to it, than any other Cornish port. The local fishing industry exported huge numbers of hogsheads of pilchards to the Spanish and Italian markets. Block tin from the rich mines of the hinterland, too heavy to take to the London dealers by road, was shipped up the English Channel, while copper ore went round Lands End to South Wales for smelting. Many luxuries arrived from the Continent and the new colonies, and essentials such as salt, coal and iron, and, for the maintenance of ships – hemp, canvas, cordage and tar. Of major importance for a comparatively treeless county, timber, in all its forms, for barrel making, housebuilding, and the mining and shipbuilding industries, was imported in vast amounts from Scandinavia and elsewhere. The tidal pools of the Bar, below Arwenack. were ideal for the storage and seasoning of baulks of timber dropped overboard from ships anchored in the Inner Harbour and rafted in. Small fishing craft would have been built in the local creeks for centuries, and there is little doubt that local skills would have played a part in the construction of the first Falmouth-built ship, of 70 or 80 tons, which was launched in August 1668. The original letter, to an unknown recipient, reporting this event also gives tantalising glimpses of Falmouth's trade, including exports of 'pilchers' (pilchards) to the Mediterranean. (*Public Record Office SP29/245*).

Sr.

Capt Trelawney of ye Georg of London from Lisbon laden with salt went hence last evening for Plimouth. Yesterday one Capt Comfort of ye Thomas of London came into this port. There are other vessels from London to lade pilchers bound for ye streights, as Capt Alderman, Neales, and Crispe, some 2 or 3 french men laden with salt, with other small vessells of the port and others outward bound. On Friday last in ye evening a new vessell of some 80, or 90 tuns, 6 gunns, being ye first ever built on this strand, was launcht, and came off very well in ye view of neare 2000 people. She is a well built ship, and called by ye name of ye Falmouth Frigatt

I am

Yours to command

Francis Bellatt

Pendennis August

ye 31th 1668

Some aspects of the life of the port at this time can be visualised by studying the letters of Penryn merchant Valentine Enys, whose letter book has been researched and edited by June Palmer. Enys, one of a number of English and Irish merchants based in the Canary Isles, was forced back to England in 1702 by the War of Spanish Succession. He continued his business from a house built by his father in Penryn, not far from the great Enys Estate to the north of the town. His transactions as a merchant and factor emphasise

Ketch *Regina* at Killigrew's quay, *c.*1920. The old Customs House with Harbour Master's office is to the left of the Globe Hotel. Other inns, the Seamen's Bethel, merchants and agents offices were in close proximity. The 49-ton *Regina* was built at Milford Haven in 1897 and was typical of the merchant vessels visiting the basin over the centuries. (RCPS.)

Ancient properties lining Falmouth High Street around 1910, viewed from the seaward-side. They are built on natural rock and amazing dry-stone walling which has supported them for centuries. (RCPS.)

Smithick Hill, 1936. As the town developed, lanes of stone and cob cottages were built on the slopes above the waterfront. Conditions were so cramped that residents ingeniously adopted ship-rigging methods to dry the washing. Long 'gaffs' were fixed to outside walls by which articles could be hoisted high above passers-by. (RCPS.)

the importance of Falmouth Harbour as a safe haven and distribution port for a wide variety of cargoes to and from the Mediterranean and the Americas. There was also busy traffic between European ports, considerably reduced during the French and Spanish Wars. At times one may have heard the speech of mariners from countries as far apart as Norway, Holland, Portugal, Italy, Wales and Ireland. Hazards for merchant ships increased considerably during hostilities, and privateering in particular went into overdrive on all sides. Owners of vessels belonging to harbours throughout the British Isles could apply to commission them as armed privateers, thereby being licensed to capture enemy merchantmen and bring them to a home port as prizes. For instance, according to figures compiled by David Starkey, between 1777 and 1782 Falmouth ships held twenty-six commissions, and of other local ports, Gweek held four , Helford two, Penryn three, and Truro two. Many a small ship on legitimate business might be captured and taken to a foreign port and its cargo confiscated, or held, with the crew, until an agreed ransom had been paid. Sometimes a ship may have been released only to be captured by a privateer from another nation as it continued on its voyage, incurring another ransom, if the owners could afford it, or seizure of the ship and an uncertain future for the crew. Worse still, ships could be captured by Barbary pirates and the crews made into galley slaves. Some ships used by Enys had been previously taken as prizes and purchased by English mariners or perhaps a consortium of merchants.

Those that know remote Gweek, on the Lizard Peninsula to the west of Falmouth, may be surprised that it once harboured privateering vessels manned by local mariners. Helston lost its own harbour in the thirteenth century when the estuary of the River Cober was cut off from the sea by the daunting barrier of shingle bank known as Loe

Bar. Thereafter Gweek, the tiny port at the head of the Helford River less than 5km away, became the town's main outlet for sea-borne trade. The coinage town exported its tin through Gweek for centuries; there were resident harbour and customs officials, and fishing and trading vessels were based on the river. A document survives relating to local mariners venturing forth in a small vessel, probably a lugger, as privateers at a time when the English Channel was thick with hostile ships from France and Spain. The capture of a valuable cargo was worth the risk when families on shore might be near starvation.

On 18 January 1781 Joseph Banfield, merchant and banker of Falmouth, wrote out a document on behalf of Captain Edward Randle of Cadgwith, confirming that a warrant had been granted to Randle for Letters of Marque:

> …for the apprehending seizing and taking the ships vessels and goods belonging to the subjects of the States General of the United Provinces or their vassals and subjects or others inhabiting within the Countries Territories or Dominions (the United Provinces consisted basically of Holland, but the wording implies that French vessels could be fair game) …the said Edward Randle's ship is called the Cadgwith is belonging to the Port of Gweek is of the burthen of 40 tons … and has 3 masts' (she has no carriage or swivel guns, but) '…is navigated with 20 men has 20 small arms 20 cutlasses 15 barrels of powder …20 weight of small shot that the said ship is victualled for 6 months has 2 suits of sails 3 anchors 3 cables and about 500 weight of spare cordage that John Johnson goes mate or lieutenant John Jacks gunner James Job boatswain Job Jarrens carpenter Jacob Jurpus (?) cook and David Damaras surgeon of the said ship and that Captain Edward Randle of Cadgwith in the County of Cornwall is the principle owner and setter out of the said ship.' *(PRO, HCA 26/56 folio 102-103)*.

During the wars with France and Spain, attempts were made to protect English merchantmen from the predation of privateers. Ships sailing from the Mediterranean and Portugal would hope to meet and receive protection from armed East Indiamen arriving in the Western Approaches where hostile ships lurked. Ships sailed in convoy whenever possible, even if it meant a long delay in port waiting to be escorted by an English man-of-war, if and when one was available. In the early eighteenth century this particularly applied to the ships carrying tin which had been coined (assayed) at Helston and Truro. Under a contract sanctioned by Queen Anne, cargoes of block tin were carried by local ships from the little ports of Gweek (for Helston) and Malpas (for Truro) to Falmouth to meet frigates of the navy to escort them through the English Channel to London. The local ships returned home with cargoes of general merchandise from the London markets, perhaps trading with intermediate ports such as Portsmouth and Plymouth en route. Voyages could take months, depending on the hazards of adverse winds, storms and enemy attack. It has been estimated that a quarter of all such ships never reached their destination. Even so, the chance had to be taken, there were profits to be made, and some insurance available for valuable cargoes. The alternative of taking heavy goods from Cornwall to London on unmade tracks by pack horse or creaking wagons drawn by oxen was not practical, especially in winter-time.

One of the official bills of lading dated 3 August 1704, concerned with the above royal contract exists in the County Record Office. Three merchants, John Mounstown (?), Richard Enys (Valentine's younger brother), and Robert Corker, are given as "Her

The quay at Market Strand, prior to the building of the first pier in 1871. This is the site of Smithick, the fishing hamlet which developed into the town of Falmouth. (RCPS.)

Majestie's Agents for the tynn contract in Cornwall". (At the time Richard Enys also held the important post of overseer of the coinage of tin in Cornwall.) The cargo consisted of 540 blocks of tin, weighing 82 tons, shipped on the *John* of Falmouth, Master Barker Tillott, "now riding at anchor in the harbour of Falmouth and by God's Grace bound for London with Convoy" and to be delivered in good order to Master Warden and Comptroller of Her Majestie's mint in the Tower of London, he paying freight charges of 25 shillings per ton "and so God send the good ship to her desired port in safety. Amen."

In his 1602 *Survey of Cornwall*, Richard Carew vividly describes the production of tin, from the time the ore is broken out of the lode or washed from the stream, to when it was turned into block tin and assayed. All processes often required extreme manual labour, performed by men, women and children under conditions which at times were akin to slave labour. Although the Cornish miners were free, the majority toiled for wages that barely kept them and their families alive. They seldom benefited from any profits made by the speculators, tinners and blowing house (smelting furnace) proprietors, a situation succinctly commented upon by Carew when discussing blowing house workers. 'I know not whether you would more marvel either whence a sufficient gain should arise to countervail so manifold expenses, or that any gain could train men to undertake such pains and peril.' After various crushing processes the refined 'black tin' was smelted:

> Then doth each man carry his portion to the blowing-house, where the same is melted with
> charcoal fire, blown by a great pair of bellows moved with a waterwheel, and so cast into
> pieces of a long and thick squareness, from three hundred to four hundred pound weight,
> at which time the owner's mark is set thereupon. The last remove is to the place of coinage,

… how great the charge the tinner undergoeth before he can bring his ore to this last mill, whereto if you add his care and cost in buying wood for the service, in felling, framing and piling it to be burned, in fetching the same when it is coaled (turned into charcoal), through such far, foul, and cumbersome ways to the blowing-house...

Until more advanced furnaces were developed in the early eighteenth century, charcoal was essential for tin smelting. Carew intimates that there were already problems obtaining supplies locally: trees do not grow well in Cornwall, and few woodlands would have escaped the search for timber to be used in the mining industry and for domestic fuel. There were some coppice woods in sheltered valleys and peat was also used as fuel and turned into charcoal for the blowing houses. However, as new sources of tin were discovered, supplies of charcoal had to be sought elsewhere. According to research on the Port Books by Dr James Whetter, for much of the seventeenth century Fal ports received cargoes of charcoal aboard coasting vessels from Southampton. This was being produced on a large scale in the New Forest, some also probably going to the Sussex iron industry. For instance, in 1635-6 ships based at Ryde and Lymington on the Isle of Wight brought into Penryn timber in the form of boards, staves and hoops, and seven cargoes of charcoal, each of 500 sacks. In the summer of 1640 several small ships from Ryde, operating for Southampton merchants, delivered to Truro a total of fifteen separate cargoes of timber in various forms and about 5,000 sacks, packs or quarters of charcoal. In 1667-8 Truro imported 9,600 sacks of charcoal, the Ryde ships returning with tin. That same year other exports of tin from Truro included forty cargoes to Plymouth and twenty to London. Falmouth-based vessels now involved in these voyages included *Bettye*, *Hopewell* and *Sarah and Dorothy*. The *Falmouth Frigatt*, reported to have been launched near the end of August 1668, is recorded in the Port Books as carrying tin to London a week after the launch, although this needs further research into the original documents as there are earlier confusing references to a vessel of the same name. In 1686 alone, Falmouth received the massive total of 56,200 sacks of charcoal. At this time Southampton was also sending timber and bricks to Falmouth and Truro, although that timber trade was probably small compared to Scandinavian imports. Coal shipments were also arriving from Swansea, Neath and Milford, the ships returning to South Wales and Bristol with copper ore. This trade was to increase over the next two centuries as coal-consuming steam engines came to dominate the mining landscape. Overseas shipments also continued to grow when war did not interrupt trade. Ships arrived from Ireland, the Low Countries, France and from across the Atlantic, Falmouth becoming one of the main importers and re-distributors of tobacco.

The earlier antagonism of Penryn towards the establishment of a custom house at Falmouth seems to have diminished by Enys's time. He considered that the two functioned as one for trading purposes; the aim was to pay as little duty as possible, preferably none at all. Various ploys were used, such as hiding valuable items for export to Portugal among ships stores or officers baggage on the packet ships 'by stealth'. The custom officials couldn't afford to upset the merchant class by being too strict, for the prosperity of the country depended on exports, and the local gentry certainly couldn't do without their imported wines. Enys organised the collection of processed pilchards from many locations

Falmouth Inner Harbour in 1819, viewed towards Penryn from the slopes of Pendennis Castle. Falmouth parish church, the town quay and Arwenack are to the left. The artist has carefully depicted the ship on the left with topmasts struck, indicating that it was probably undergoing repairs on the Bar. (Cornwall Centre.)

along the Cornish coast, to be sent as far as Italy and to his old friends in the Canaries, from whence his ships returned with Canary wine. This was sold on to various contacts, perhaps in Bristol, Exeter or London, sometimes after some necessary doctoring by local vintners. A major import from other sources was barrel staves for making the various types of containers, such as pilchard hogsheads and wine pipes.

Merchants such as Enys dealt with any commodity which would turn a profit, requiring communications with a very wide circle of contacts for the distribution of goods by land and sea. Apart from wine and pilchards, Falmouth and Penryn quays were dealing with tobacco, rum and sugar from the Americas, timber from the Baltic nations, Atlantic cod and herrings, cloth from Holland and Spain, and wine from Portugal and Northern Italy. A major import was salt for processing and preserving pilchards and other foods. Enys also organised the collection of foodstuffs such as bread and peas from local suppliers for victualling the packet ships. The vessels visiting Falmouth in the early years of the eighteenth century included big three-masted transatlantic East Indiamen, English men-of-war, Dutch privateers and captured prizes of various kinds, some of the latter probably refitted in the harbour as English merchantmen, and also 'gallys', described below. Typical trading ships of the period would have been two-masted square-rigged brigs, of perhaps only 40 or 50 tons, similar in appearance to the larger, faster and better-armed packet ships based in the harbour.

Enys used the term 'gally' for about a dozen different vessels in his correspondence, several being based in the harbour and used by him and other merchants for cargo-carrying. These were not the lightly built fighting galleys of the Mediterranean, with lateen sails and banks of oars manned by slaves, a similar type also built by Peter the Great for

The brig *Nautilus*, a 500-ton Royal Navy vessel built at Pembroke Dock in 1879 and later used as a boys training vessel attached to the *Impregnable* at Devonport and probably the *Ganges* at Falmouth. She was sold to Cox & Co. of Falmouth in 1905 and broken up. Similar vessels were built in Falmouth in the early nineteenth century. (RCPS.)

the Russian navy, and adapted elsewhere in Europe. There were several similar-sounding terms allied to 'galley' for various cargo-carrying vessels, such as the galeass of the Baltic, and the galiot, a small versatile craft which is said to have originated in the Netherlands, used in transatlantic voyages as well as coastal work. This latter type seems the most likely candidate for the Enys gallys. In 1667, after previously being involved in the hazards of part-ownership of a privateer, Samuel Pepys is said to have acquired a King's ship, the galiot *Maybolt*, for use as a merchantman: the type was therefore already well known to English seafarers. In the eighteenth century, galiots of the North Sea area were equipped with two masts, with fore- and aft-rigged main and mizzen sails, several jibs, and square- rigged sails on the main mast, a sort of hybrid between a schooner and ketch. The average galiot varied in length between 18-30m and a beam between 4-7½m, with a carrying capacity of up to 130 tons. Needing only a small crew of four or five, or perhaps more if armed, a craft such as this would have been ideal for fast commercial voyages to the Mediterranean or the Canary Isles, and can be thought of as a precursor of the merchant schooners.

The Enys letters not only shed light on many aspects of Falmouth and Penryn's maritime trade but also reveal something of the lives of his contemporaries in and around the harbour. One gentleman in particular, a leading figure in the history of the Bar, was John Netherton, who, it is revealed, not only built a tide mill there (discussed later), but was also a shipbuilder, and, being leaseholder, the logical place for him to build a ship was on the shores of the Bar. John Netherton possibly originated in the Plymouth area and moved to Falmouth in about 1668, leasing the Bar in 1671, and becoming a prominent citizen, being a church warden and several times mayor of the infant town. Two of his daughters married packet ship captains and another married the naval officer Captain Richard Upton, who leased Arwenack Manor House. In 1701 Netherton was said to be a shipwright aged fifty-six years, and in 1707 he was commissioned to go to Scilly to inspect and try to salvage the now famous wreck of Sir Cloudesley Shovell's flagship the *Association*. John Netherton is still leaseholder of the Bar in 1725, when he would have been eighty years old. According to the parish registers, he died the following year, having far outlived his first-born son, John Jnr, who had died in 1709.

From 1704 Valentine Enys was involved in protracted negotiations regarding the purchase of a new ship being built by Netherton; the construction location is not known, however the obvious place is the Bar. Letters by Enys to prospective purchasers, merchants in Portugal and England, gave the dimensions of a substantial craft, with a construction strong enough to support up to twelve guns. It was thought good enough to be put in use as a privateer, Netherton, 'the ship carpenter', judging it would outsail the packet ships. Enys measured the keel length at 61ft (18.6m); the overall length seems to have been 75ft (23m). Depth in the hold was 9ft (2.75m), with a cramped 3.5ft (1.07m) height between decks, 'which makes 140 tons'. At that period the calculation of tonnage was worked out by using a multiple of 'tuns', which were casks of wine, holding, in modern terms, 252 gallons, otherwise two pipes, or four hogsheads. Until 1982 a registered tonnage was calculated using multiples of 100cu.ft of internal capacity. A variety of measurements had been used in Britain and abroad over the centuries. The comprehensive fitting out inventory was to include at least two masts, sails, rope, blocks, anchors, pumps, compasses, iron-work for chain plates and rudder, two boats, and defensive small arms. One proposed captain had even managed to obtain cheap cutlasses, ball, powder and grenades. The crew's well-being was also considered: dishes, plates, spoons and ladles being provided and allowance made for four months provisions for a crew of thirty, a similar number to that of the packet ships. The ship's name was to be the *Sea Nymph*. Two years later the sale still had not been completed; Enys had probably invested in two eighth shares and was still trying to persuade others.

One owner was to be the foremost Falmouth merchant Robert Corker, who appears to have been a ruthless businessman, for years in conflict with the Killigrew family. Corker never seems to have paid Enys fully for his share of the ship; the executors of both were still wrangling over settlement after their deaths. Robert Corker had become apprentice to merchant Bryan Rogers in 1682. He turned out to be a cuckoo in the nest; by his early twenties, through ruthless business practices, he had virtually taken over his benefactor's firm. On the death of Rogers in 1693 he also took over his house, allegedly turning the widow out with little ceremony. He soon became the dominant export merchant in the area. Meanwhile, according to Tattersfield (see Bibliography), his younger brother Thomas had become apprentice in the London-based Royal Africa Company, which sought to monopolise trade to Sierra Leone and Guinea. Much of their trade consisted of the export from England of manufactured goods, including guns, to coastal trading forts,

Early nineteenth-century shipbuilding. An engraving by J. J. Baugean.

there to be bartered for exotic woods, gold, ivory and slaves, the latter being sent on the hellish transatlantic journey to the Caribbean sugar plantations. In Africa, for a number of years Thomas Corker was in his element (he was an exception: most Europeans that were sent out, including many prospective gold miners from Cornwall, didn't survive for long). Within a few years, far away from his London superiors, he built up his own trading empire. He seems to have been even more unscrupulous than his brother, his methods making him almost universally disliked.

Although the Company prohibited such practice, in the 1690s Thomas imported barter goods from England and exported slaves on his own account, the financial arrangements in Cornwall being handled by brother Robert in Falmouth. For malpractice over a number of years Thomas was eventually dismissed by the Company and returned to Falmouth in 1700; he was a sick man, and died, aged only thirty-one, in September of that year. Sometime later the Company began proceedings to recover a share of his substantial estate from his mother and brother. In 1701 Robert Corker made his own speculation in the Guinea trade: he sent through Falmouth customs a cargo of beads, cloth, iron and metalware, which were put on board the Gambia-bound ship *Thomas*. Apparently, the captain traded successfully: gold and slave trading was almost certainly involved. Corker suddenly became richer, and was also able to present his mother with the gift of a black girl of sixteen, who was later baptised in Falmouth parish church. Corker used some of his profits to invest in four privateers, one being Netherton's *Sea Nymph*, which, in 1710, justified the shipwright's earlier confidence by capturing a Turkish vessel, the *Holy Cross*, in the Mediterranean. The only other voyage on record was previously in 1707, when the ship sailed as a merchantman to Virginia, when it was then known as the *Falmouth Gally*.

The Killigrew Monument, the Submarine Pier and Grove Place Beach, possibly in the 1930s. The 12m-high obelisk was originally sited in the gardens of the manor house, later moved to the hillside towards Pendennis and to its present position in 1871. (RCPS.)

Peter Killigrew died in 1705, far away from Arwenack, the house having been rented out five years previously. He was the last of the male line: his only son, George, had been tragically killed in a duel in Penryn. A Martin Lister married Ann, the youngest daughter, taking the name of Killigrew, and, plagued with disputes with the borough officials, administered the estate to the best of his ability, mainly from London. Martin wrote a history of the Killigrews, and built the Pyramid, the lasting memorial to the family, originally set up in the grounds of the manor and now standing sentinel in front of the much altered house. The inheritance passed, via the second daughter, Francis, to the Wodehouse family, the third baron becoming the Earl of Kimberley in 1866.

Daniel Defoe, in his masterly work *A Tour through the Whole Island of Great Britain*, provides much information on the economic life of the county during the first decades of the eighteenth century. However, going by some of the distances he gives between places, one wonders if he actually travelled the routes. Quite possibly he used material provided by local informants in some areas, although generally his descriptions are thought to be sound.

The town of Falmouth is by much the richest, and best trading town in this county, though not so ancient as its neighbour town of Truro ,.... Falmouth has gotten the trade, at least the best part of it from the other, which is chiefly owing to the situation, for that Falmouth lying upon the sea, but within the entrance, ships of the greatest burthen come up to the very quays, and the whole royal navy might ride safely in the road .... Falmouth is well built, has abundance of shipping belonging to it, is full of rich merchants, and has a flourishing and increasing trade. I say increasing, because by the late setting up the English packets between

The Town or Custom House Quay, *c.*1920. Vessels have been using the basin for shelter or transfer of cargoes for over three centuries. Falmouth quay punts are at their moorings beyond the narrow entrance. (RCPS.)

Some of the Penzance lugger fleet in the basin, probably on a Sunday when by tradition no fishing was allowed, *c.*1900. (RCPS.)

The basin possibly around 1920. By this time some of the fishing craft had the luxury of engines and wheel-houses. Three Penzance boats are moored bows-on to North Quay alongside a smart trading smack and three-masted schooner which is discharging cargo into the waiting cart. (RCPS.)

this port and Lisbon, there is a new commerce between Portugal and this town, carried on to a very great value. It is true, part of this trade was founded in a clandestine commerce, carried on by the said packets....

During the eighteenth century, Falmouth became known to men of commerce throughout many parts of the world as the packet service expanded to the Mediterranean, West Indies, and North and South America. A century after its foundation there were t wenty-two Falmouth-based vessels employed in the service, a number which had almost doubled in the first decades of the nineteenth century. Shipyard facilities in the port had to expand not only to build and service the packets, but also for the growing merchant fleet. According to figures in the Public Record Office researched by Willan on the total tonnage of coastal vessels (not packets or large ships) belonging to Cornish ports, in 1709 Falmouth's tonnage was given as 60 tons, perhaps comprising two ships, whereas by 1751 this figure had grown to 571 tons. In comparison, other ports such as Fowey and Padstow began the century with more coasting craft, but didn't increase their tonnage over the same period: Fowey averaged about 300 tons and Padstow about 650. Padstow had a comparatively large fleet because of its local trade with Ireland, South Wales, Bristol and the Severn ports.

Since the foundation of Falmouth four centuries ago, its harbour has proved of strategic importance on the Western Approaches to the English Channel. Protected by Pendennis and St Mawes Castles, and in more recent conflicts by batteries on St Anthony Head,

The basin in the 1970s. By then the inshore fleet mainly consisted of motor launches, but which still carried steadying mizzen sails. Merchant vessels have rarely discharged cargoes here since the Second World War. (RCPS.)

in time of war it has provided a refuge and victualling base from the Age of Raleigh to the twentieth century. Its Victorian-built docks, enlarged and modernised with changing requirements, have been vital for the repair of ships through two world wars, and Falmouth's location has been equally important for the maritime commerce of Cornwall and of Britain. While ocean-going ships plied in and out of the Port of Falmouth, in numerous creeks and on the foreshores of the Fal, Penryn and Perquil Rivers, generations of skilled shipwrights of working boats and small sailing vessels carried on their trade. Of some yards perhaps nothing remains except a few posts and a broken stone quay; a few locations are still occupied with shipwrights able to work in traditional wood as well as modern materials. Some sites have disappeared altogether, no more so than at the Bar, once an area of thriving maritime industry at the southern end of the Falmouth water-front, where, long before the docks existed, and for a time afterwards, small shipyards built and repaired countless craft. In the centre of the activity, the Bar corn mills quietly ground away, in the most environmentally friendly manner, producing flour to help feed the population.

TWO

THE HARBOUR MILLS

OF MILLS IN GENERAL

Although most of the nucleated settlements of Saxon England had their manorial mills by the time of the Domesday Survey of 1086, there were only a handful of watermills recorded for the sparsely populated lands of Cornwall. However, throughout the rapid development of post-medieval mining for tin and copper in the mineral areas, the Cornish used marvellous ingenuity to utilise every small rivulet, of which there were plenty, to turn waterwheels to drive labour-saving machinery. People also have to eat, and as the population grew, many mills were built to grind corn to make bread. Wheat flour was available to all when harvests were good, although in bad years the poor were reduced to eating barley bread. Animal feed stuffs also had to be ground and stored for winter use. In the Fal catchment alone, that is on streams which empty into the estuary, at one time or another there were over thirty water-driven corn mills operating. Because the streams were generally small, all had *overshot* wheels, whereby water is fed via a long leat to the top of the wheel, which is turned by the weight of water flowing into the buckets. There were also a few windmills on hills around the Fal, even a post mill as early as the seventeenth century within the fortifications of Pendennis Castle. But because of the unpredictability, and sometimes violence of the winds, all were short-lived compared to watermills.

Tides are predictable: as long as there is a moon above, they will rise and fall in a regular cycle. Therefore, from early times, where there is a good tidal range, people have dammed tidal creeks to pen a *head* of sea water within a dam to drive waterwheels to grind corn. These mills utilised *undershot*, rarely *breastshot*, wheels, whereby at low tide a sluice gate is lifted and the force of the water flowing from above the dam strikes the *floats* or paddles on the wheel to make it revolve. There were a great variety of tide mills, sometimes referred to as sea mills, around the coasts of Europe: many still stand, few are working. Off the north coast of Brittany, on Ile de Bréhat, an island with no streams to speak of, there is a delightful small seventeenth-century mill built of the beautiful local pink granite. Tides are of some magnitude here, and the dam is high. The eight-armed wheel

Ile de Bréhat, Brittany 2005. A restored example of a seventeenth-century tide mill similar to those once working on the Bar. The view is from the top of the enormous dam at low tide. The pool is on the right, although no water has been retained in it.

Ile de Bréhat mill wheel. The narrow deceptively primitive-looking wooden wheel would have generated considerable power from the narrow mill race below it.

is made of wood, with thirty-two floats; some of the Cornish mills may have been of similar simple design. The larger surviving mills in Britain have variously designed wheels, sometimes more than one, often inside the building. These include Bromley-by-Bow on the River Lea, French mill at Carew Castle, Pembrokeshire, and Eling (pronounced 'Eeling'), on a creek off Southampton Water. The latter is the only one which produces flour, albeit on a part-time basis for visitors. Another which cannot be left out is the white-painted, timber-clad mill at Woodbridge on the River Deben in Suffolk. It has an oak-built 6m wheel, which is set in motion, depending on tide times, for the benefit of summer visitors. Its comparatively rural setting has been somewhat marred, as the mill pond is now a marina.

In his *Survey of Cornwall*, published in 1602, Richard Carew remarks on the damming of tidal creeks to work undershot grist mills. Known sites, of varying date of use, include several on each of the Rivers Lynher and Camel, and the harbours at West Looe and Hayle. At the latter, the mill was constructed to provide animal feed for horses employed in the industrial works. On the Fal Estuary in the eighteenth century there was a tide corn mill at the head of Mylor Creek, and a nineteenth century bone-crushing mill at Penpol. At the latter site the tidal pool is so restricted and shallow it is hard to believe that a waterwheel could have operated here. However, at both Mylor and Penpol there are small streams in the valleys behind, which may have augmented the tidal pool levels. At Place House, opposite to St Mawes Harbour on the Percuil River, a great ornamental dam at the head of Place Creek marks the site of a milldam, the lawn behind it once being the millpool. John Leland saw this mill in about 1538 during his travels through the county, and sometime later Boazio marked the dam on his chart. In 1726, George Spry, owner of Place House, leased St Anthony corn or grist mill to Richard Pierce of St Mawes for £90 yearly. The property was advertised to let in the *West Briton* on 27 May 1812. It included 25 acres of land, fishing rights, and the benefits of sand and shingle from the foreshore. Admiral Thomas Spry leased it to John Luke of St Anthony the following year. Apparently it was demolished in about 1860.

Further along the Percuil River, at the head of the beautiful Porth Creek, Froe Tide mill was constructed as late as 1808. The reason for what seems a speculative venture is unclear: it is unlikely that there had been a large bread-consuming population increase in this remote area! It was first advertised for sale by auction on 25 March 1809 in the *Royal Cornwall Gazette*. The property consisted of a large dwelling house, a walled garden and small area of land. One promoted advantage was that it was 'desirably situated for any person wishing to embark in the coal or timber trade'. A coal wharf here would have been advantageous to the residents of Gerrans parish; the existing wharf at Place in St Anthony was 2km further away. The depth of water in Porth Creek, especially at spring tide high water, seems sufficient for the shallow-draughted Fal barges to have reached a wharf situated at the end of the creek and adjacent road, although a wharf was never built. The mills (meaning one wheel driving two pairs of stones) are '…erected on such a construction as to be rarely equalled'. That statement is certainly true – although the mill building is no longer there (it may have been timber-built), the great stone-walled dam, complete with tide and wheel sluice apertures, is as intact as when it was built two centuries ago. It has alternating sections of vertical and horizontal drystone walling of the

Froe Tide mill dam, 2005, pictured from the mill pool, with Porth Creek and St Mawes beyond. The tide inlet sluice aperture (much altered) is to the left. The site of the mill is behind the trees to the right.

Detail of the dry-stone walling of Froe Tide mill dam, from the seaward side.

local killas rock, probably with a rubble core. At the time of the Tithe Apportionment of 1840 the mill was occupied by William Dowrick: that apart, little is known of its history.

Also on the Percuil River which he calls 'St Mawes Creek', Leland noted another mill: 'St Mawes Creek is tidal for the first two miles inland to the east–north–east and at the limit of the tidal creek there is a mill powered by a freshwater stream which flows into it...' This was probably Trethem mill, near St Just-in-Roseland. However, there is another finger of the Percuil River, Polingey Creek, in Gerrans parish, which could be a contender for Lelands' second mill. A 'Sea Mill' is indicated here on the Ordnance Survey map of 1813, the pool, like Penpol and Mylor mills, supplemented by a valley stream. Hilary Thompson, in the first of her books on the history of Gerrans, writes that the property was described in 1853 as consisting of a small house of three rooms and two garrets and a single grist mill with one pair of stones. The miller prior to 1820 (when he was drowned while returning from Falmouth) was Henry Merifield. A Joshua Rosevear took over in 1834. It is recorded in the Gerrans Tithe Apportionment of 1841 as having a 4-acre pool, and with the surrounding land was then occupied by John Penhallow Esq. It is also depicted on the six-inch Ordnance Survey map of 1908 as a small structure at the centre of a mill dam, although, according to Thompson, in 1861 it was already unoccupied. Nothing remains of it apart from the stumps of a double row of stone-work across the creek and a small island exposed at low water.

THE BAR POOLS

In 1693 the hydrographer Captain Greenvile Collins published the first reasonably accurate pilot charts of the coastline of Great Britain. His chart of the Fal was sponsored by Sir Peter Killigrew the Second. With depths measured in fathoms, it may have been of some use to ships of the day, but is of no use to present mariners. If Collins' measurements were accurate, it indicates that over the last three centuries there have been considerable changes in the position of sandbanks in the estuary. Off Pendennis, the Bar Point bank, shown by Boazio as a long thin tongue, is depicted by Collins as a large area of shallows extending nearly as far as the Arwenack shore: however, those particular features on both charts served the same purpose – Mariners – Keep Away! Collins paid particular attention to the Arwenack Bar area, for the single pool (if the Burghley map is to be relied upon) of a century before had now became two. Beside each pool Collins has drawn his symbol for a building. At least one of the buildings, probably both, represents a tide mill.

It is obvious that the rapidly expanding seventeenth-century population of Falmouth needed to have a reliable source of flour for making bread, which would have formed a large portion of their diet: ships visiting the port would also have needed victualling. Several small local mills probably produced enough flour and animal feed for the small scattered communities in Budock and Arwenack manors. Penryn also had several mills, but knowing of the animosity between the two towns, it is unlikely that Falmouth bakers could have purchased flour from them. It is therefore possible that Peter Killigrew, the First or Second, initially leased out part of the tidal pool area known as the Bar for the erection of tide-powered corn mills to increase food production for the town. In about 1672 Peter Killigrew the Second is said to have obtained the advice of the great Dutch engineer Cornelius Vermuyden regarding the building of a mill in the town, and at the same time provide a water supply for ships at the quay. Mill buildings were erected and water obtained via a leat across country from Kergilliack. After heavy investment in the project, Sir Peter's scheme was thwarted, allegedly by a certain Brian Rogers, who for many years

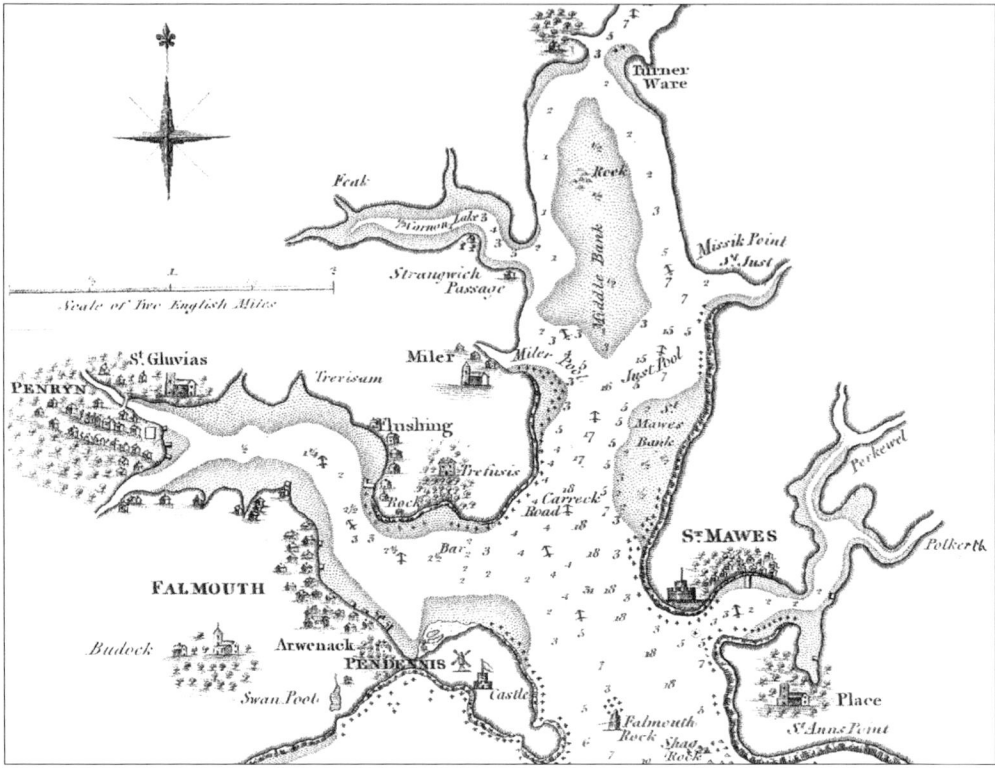

The southern section of Greenvile Collins' chart of 1693, copied for *A Historical Survey of Cornwall* by C.S. Gilbert, 1817. 'Carnon Lake' represents Restronguet; 'Perkewel' is Percuil (towards Polingey); and 'Polkerth' is Porth Creek. Arwenack Bar is to the left of the post mill at Pendennis Castle. (Cornwall Centre.)

controlled the town council, and was a bitter opponent of the Killigrews. It is perhaps significant that several years later Sir Peter granted leases for tide mills at the Bar.

The earliest printed historical information regarding mills at the Bar appeared in Susan E. Gay's book *Old Falmouth*, which she published in 1903. Here she states:

> Mr Thomas Banfield held in the forties a lease of the 'Barr' (Bar) mills, belonging to this Manor, as well as some land near the Castle, with the mill fields. He had mills of his own. He, however, got into difficulties and his lease of the Bar mills was taken over by Mr Bluett...

Later historians, including Rex Wailes[1], and Walter Minchinton[2], have copied this quote, assuming that Gay was referring to the 1840s. No account has been found of any Banfield 'difficulties', but, apart from that, she was referring to the 1740s! Study of the Arwenack bailiffs' books of estate leases and rents in the County Record Office reveals a more comprehensive, if somewhat complicated, history of the mills.

It is difficult to imagine how extensive were the Bar pools three centuries ago before mill dams and other development began. However, later large-scale maps, particularly the

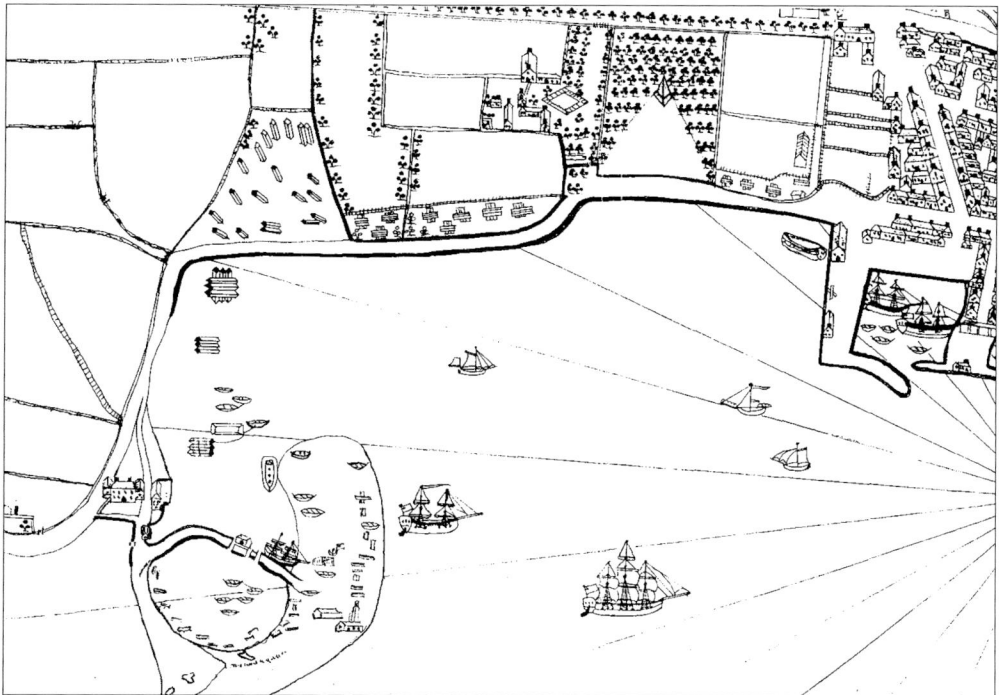

The 1773 map of Falmouth (detail): Peter Gilson's meticulous reconstruction of a unique map in the town library. (North is to the right.) Killigrew's quay is to the right; Arwenack Manor centre top; Bar House lower left, and below it is Banfield's mill on the earliest dam, its pool bottom left. Netherton's mill and dam, with prominent sluice openings, is to the right, extending to the whale-like curve of the Bar bank with its signs of shipbuilding activity. Baulks of timber are conspicuous on the foreshore, Arwenack Green, and the timber pond to its left. The latter two sites are now car parks. (RCPS.)

1773 map of Falmouth, the tithe maps, and the 1861 Docks Proposal Plan by Bertram Symons, show their original area. Apart from the small promontory, or spit of land, on which sat the Bar House (later the Dock and Railway Hotel and so on), the curving Bar Road marks the edge of the foreshore of the pools almost to where it now passes under the railway bridge. An inner pool extended nearly as far as the Dock Station buildings. The Railway Cottages, and all buildings between there and the present maritime museum, are constructed upon the filled-in pools and the sand and shingle banks of the Bar.

BANFIELD'S MILL

The first man-made alterations to the natural bar area seem to have consisted of the building (or extending) of a wide bank, probably revetted with timber piling, from (for want of a better word) the Bar House promontory, in a north-easterly direction, to join up with the natural curving outer bank. This created a large inner tidal pool, of perhaps several acres, to the west of the aforesaid promontory. A small mill and sluices were then constructed on the south-west end of the new bank next to the Bar House site. The mill is depicted, rather fancifully, on a late seventeenth-century map, the 1773 Falmouth Map, and a print by Stanfield and Cousen, around 1850, probably with much artistic licence. The existence of this mill, and its more successful neighbour, is confirmed by the Killigrew Estate leases. The brief details of some leases and rents, covering less than a century of administration, were written down in a book with the names of leaseholders in alphabetical order[3]. Most of the records are legible, but some can be confusing, as they post-date the original documents. They provide only snapshots of the history of the Bar, and their interpretation must also be treated with some caution. The earliest relevant record begins:

> Rowland Banfield by assignment of John Thomas…. of St Just ….holds Trudgeon's mills and houses by lease granted to ye said Trudgeon Bearing date 20th August 1674…

for which Banfield paid rent of one shilling and five pence, plus one capon. The full yearly value was £20. It can be deduced from this that a miller called Trudgeon, or his employee, was grinding corn on the Bar from, or perhaps for sometime before, 1674.

Rowland Banfield continued to rent this mill: in 1709 and 1711 he also paid for the '…. yearly composition of small tithes for ye year….' for Trudgeon's mills, Netherton's mills, Manor mills, Bennetts' Moores, Cliff Meadow, Upton's Barn Field and Upton's Slip Meadows. *Upton's Slip* is one of the few remaining opes (narrow passageways) in the town, which lead down to the original foreshore. It is difficult to imagine that there were once meadows here. Manor mills were the Budock manorial mills, located on a stream running into Swan Pool. The building no longer exists, and even its location is uncertain. Bennetts' Moores adjoined this mill in Swan Vale. Netherton's mills are discussed below. Cliff Meadows, also recorded as Cliff Close or Mill Close, were situated behind Bar House, and are now covered by Bar Terrace and the railway. (Confusingly, another 'Cliff Meadow' was recorded over a century later on the Tithe Map, but located in the Cliff Road area towards Gyllyngvase. It consisted of over 2-acres of arable and was leased by a Samuel Banfield, a probable descendant of the earlier Banfields.) A note of 1711 states that Rowland Banfield paid one year's rent of £33 8s to Martin Killigrew for the properties listed above. Nothing is known of the people who lived and worked, and paid rent, on these lands.

Up to about 1724, Rowland Banfield, who was an elderly gentleman by then, was still paying annual rent for Trudgeon's mills and associated fields, but by 1712 the manorial mills in Swan Vale had been taken over by his son Thomas. Another son, Joseph, is also mentioned, although Rowland seems to have still been paying that rent until 1720. Thomas Banfield was still leasing the Swan Vale properties in 1738 and it seems that, possibly on the death of his father, he had also taken over Trudgeon's mills – a 1751 lease to Bluett (discussed later) cites 'Thomas Banfield's Trudgeon's mills'. The Banfields had either a very special lease for this mill, or it was extremely unproductive, for the annual rent over many years remained fixed at only £1 5d. Later in the century a Joseph Banfield became a respected banker and merchant in the town: his relationship to the earlier Banfields is unknown.

Under a lease of 1760 William Bluett made repairs to the mill costing £30, and it was included in a lease of 1792 held by Sarah, the widow of Richard Bluett. This is the last

Joseph Farington's view of the Bar, *c.*1810. The Banfield's mill tide sluice mechanism, probably a simple hand-spike windlass, is to the left. To its right is Netherton's mill and dam, and the shipyard on the Bar. (Cornwall Centre.)

Stanfield's engraving of the town quay and church from the mill dam, date uncertain. An intriguing depiction of what could be Banfield's mill wheel, with sluice-gate operated by a hand-spike windlass. Compare the construction of the wheel with that on the Ile de Bréhat mill. (Falmouth Art Gallery.)

written record of the mill: by now it would have been of low priority compared to the family's shipbuilding interests. There is conflicting pictorial and cartographical evidence as to its later existence. The Thomas town map of 1827 does not include it, but the 1841 tithe map and an 1861 docks proposal plan show that at least the sluice apertures and the foundation platform seem to be intact. The tide sluice mechanism can be seen to the left-hand side of the Farington print of 1810, and the building seems to be intact on that by Thomas Allen dated 1831.

There is an engraving entitled *Falmouth from the Mills* by George Clarkson Stanfield, R.A., which according to an art expert is unlikely to have been produced before about 1848 (Stanfield was born in 1828). This depicts an intact waterwheel and sluice gate operated by a hand-spike windlass, the wheel being attached to a low thatched building of which only a small section can be seen. The structure is exactly on the right alignment for Banfield's mill, and it certainly doesn't represent Netherton's mill. The wheel illustrated is of an almost identical primitive design as the Ile de Bréhat mill, and is also similar to its neighbouring Netherton's mill (although the width of the latter wheel is not known). It is impossible to know what function this mill had: *if* the Stanfield engraving is a near accurate representation it could not have been very efficient. The artist may have used considerable imaginative licence or had a now derelict or demolished structure described to him by locals. Nevertheless, the mill's position, with the town quay and sailing ships in the background, plus evidence from other mills, indicates that the picture is a reasonably accurate representation of Banfield's mill. The date of its actual demise remains a mystery.

NETHERTON'S MILL

In 1671, as Peter Killigrew's new quay was under construction, he granted a lease for the large outer shingle bank of the Bar not already taken up by the Trudgeon mill development. This new property was later recorded by the estate steward thus:

> John Netherton holds by lease bearing date of 20 March 1671 Consideration of sum of three pounds and ten shillings fine then paid. Arwennack Barr, without limitation or any boundings, other than by the words (Arwennack Barr) which uncertainty of ye sett proves now troublesome and of ill consequence. This lease contains a reservation to ye leasor of liberty to build upon any part of ye said Barr, not built upon or inclosed by ye leasee…

The yearly value was given as £40. The 'ill consequence' seems to have had no future ramifications. At an unspecified date Netherton also held, by agreement a woodyard 'between two long cellars at ye key', the cellars either being pilchard processing works, or more likely warehousing for shipping using the new quay built by Sir Peter Killigrew. Under another lease, it was near here, or perhaps on the outer Bar, that Netherton constructed a long building consisting of six or more tenements, a piece of property development which was no doubt prevalent in the town, as new residents and visiting mariners sought accommodation. A lease for this 'long tenement of houses' was issued in October 1674. Netherton's next lease, the most vital to the story of the 'Bar Mill', was issued to him on 6 October 1679. It included:

….consideration a mill to be built upon ye premises …. Arwennack Barr without other boundings than in ye first lease. This lease contains ye like reservation of building by ye leasor as in ye first….

Along with his shipbuilding interests, as previously discussed, Netherton began a major project of constructing a second mill dam, requiring many barge-loads of stone, to enclose more of the tidal inlet encompassed by the outer Bar. The curving dam began next to the tidal sluices of Trudgeon's mill and reached northwards to finish midway along the outer Bar bank. The dam may have been constructed in a similar fashion to that of Froe Tide mill.

Apart from one reference in the documents to repairs or alterations in later years, it must be assumed that nineteenth- and twentieth-century illustrations of Netherton's mill and its environs depict the structure as it was first built. The solid foundation was set to the same height as the dam, above maximum (hopefully) high-tide levels. The outer facing wall on the long west side was stone built to the first floor, reinforced at the corners with dressed granite quoins. Apart from a chimney stack incorporated into the north end, the rest was timber-built. Although it would seem folly to have open fires within a timber building full of combustible materials, including flour dust, it was not an unusual feature in small mills. In the case of a tide mill, which as the cycle of tides progressed needed constant attention night and day, a bit of night-time warmth from a small fire during rest periods would be most welcome. Skilled professional millers who may have been employed by the leaseholder may even have had family accommodation within the mill. A possible alternative is that part of the upper floor could have been used for drying barley for malt production. For a time the building was known as Netherton's/Jessop's Mill, Jessop being a local maltster whose house was listed under some of the Banfield leases.

One of the earliest landscape illustrations of the Bar was published in 1814 as an engraved print of a south view of Falmouth in the Cornwall edition of Lyson's *Britannia*. The engraving was based on a sketch by Joseph Farington, R.A., and can be taken to be a reasonable accurate representation of the scene before the eye of the artist. Farington was a prolific landscape painter, many of his watercolours being used to illustrate books. One particular series of the Thames in the 1790s involved mills, navigation works and water craft and demonstrates that he was a skilled draughtsman. Farington is said to have been a mentor of William Turner, introducing his work to the Royal Academy. He was also widely travelled, and reported on many aspects of Georgian life in his copious diaries. He recorded his visit to Cornwall in September 1810, travelling by mail coach and chaise to Tehidy. He visited Falmouth on 22 September, staying at Greenbank and using the ferry to Flushing ('half the profits of the ferry belong to Lord Wodehouse'). The next day was wet – he walked to Falmouth Church for the service conducted by the Revd Hitchins (sermon forty minutes – 'the organ and singing very good'). It is on one of these days that he made his sketches of Falmouth and recorded the Bar area for posterity.

The more romantic 1831 view by Thomas Allen was sketched from a higher elevation and is unlikely to have been 'borrowed' from Farington. The latter artist has drawn a wheelhouse on Netherton's mill, whereas Allen shows an exposed wheel, otherwise the mill, shipyard buildings and fishermen's hovels on the Banfield/Trudgeon dam are

Allen's 1831 version of the then picturesque view across Banfield's mill pool. Today's Maritime Museum is situated where the brig lies on stocks. Netherton's (Bar) mill is to the left, and possibly Banfield's mill, half-hidden by the trees. (Cornwall Centre.)

similar. The mill had an unusual raised portion in the centre of the roof ridge, possibly to accommodate a sack hoist mechanism, or even louvres for ventilation. On the dam side there were two lean-tos, and another smaller one, perhaps a privy, at the north end. In the absence of evidence for an industrial use, it must be assumed that both Netherton's and Banfield's properties were corn mills, with three floors and the standard machinery within. Banfield's mill is only illustrated by symbols on a few maps, by the tide sluice windlass frame on the Farington print of 1810, and part of the building on the Allen print of 1831: however, its operation would have been similar to its neighbour. Various illustrations of Netherton's mill, later known as the Bar Mill, show the apertures in the dam at either end of the building. The northern one had a one-way sea gate which automatically swung open on the flood tide to allow the sea to fill the mill pool, in similar fashion to the mill on the Ile de Bréhat. It closed at high tide to retain the *head* of water in the pool.

The southern aperture contained the wheel sluice gate, which when raised allowed water in the pool onto the wheel. There is only one simple close-up view, by an unknown artist, which gives some idea of the construction of the wheel. Assuming that it is portrayed to the best of the artist's ability, and comparison with other views confirm that it is, the wheel had six single or pairs of arms, these, the axle and rim, probably oak-built. The thirty or so paddles or floats were most likely made of elm, a timber not as strong as oak, but more resilient and less inclined to rot in water. The axle was supported on its outer bearing by a retaining wall, against which were steps for maintenance, such as greasing and balancing. On the wheel axle extending behind the mill wall there would have been a large, cogged pit wheel, from which was driven all the mill machinery. The

Bar Mill, *c.* 1850. Artist unknown. (RCPS.)

gap between the bottom edges of the moving floats and the stone cill below the sluice gate was as narrow as possible to create maximum efficiency. Therefore there would have been a grill above the sluice to stop large objects shooting through, which could jam beneath and smash the floats.

'Time and tide wait for no man' might well be applied to tide mill operation. At high tide much of the wheel would be covered by the sea. As the tide ebbed, the wheel was gradually uncovered, and as it dropped below axle level the wheel could be turned, but with considerable drag. Proper milling usually only commenced when the floats were more or less clear of the ebbing sea level. Then the sluice gate was raised just high enough for a wide jet of water from the pool to drive with considerable force onto the bottom floats to set the wheel in motion. According to information from existing working tide mills, it is estimated that grinding could be undertaken for five to six hours before the tide returned enough to stop the wheel and start refilling the pool. There were considerable variations in proceedure between spring and neap tides.

Up to at least 1725 John Netherton was paying annual rent of £4 8*s* for various properties, including his Arwenack Bar, and the mill he had built about forty-five years before.

A chalk and charcoal sketch by Robert Collinson, *c.*1880. Bar Mill from across the mill pool, with schooners in Bar Creek, showing piling and sluice apertures of the dam. (Falmouth Art Gallery.)

THE BLUETT LEASES

According to Susan E. Gay, the ancient land-owning family of Bluett, or Blewett, was, and still is, 'scattered about' in Cornwall. A local branch owned the Trevethan Estate which once existed on the north side of the present Falmouth town, one resident being Captain Francis Bluett, second husband of Jane Killigrew. Among the leases issued for property in the rapidly expanding town was one to a Richard Bluett, dated 25 March 1704:

> Consideration ye rent to be paid and building to be erected. He holds his estate … 36 foot
> in front … bounded to ye north by ye new way leading down to ye key …. to ye east by ye
> wall of ye key work to be built by Sir Peter Killigrew … and to ye west by ye street...

In modern parlance this would be called a prime piece of real estate! It is likely that at this time new quay works and sea defences were proceeding all along the waterfront. Three years later Richard was paying rent for a dwelling house and land, almost certainly for the aforementioned property near the quay; in 1711 the lease was under the name of John Bluett.

It is not known what business this branch of the family followed at the time, almost certainly it was shipbuilding. Whatever the trade, it was lucrative: on 25 December 1751 William, perhaps a son of Richard or John, was wealthy enough to take a lease for the whole Arwenack Bar area, including 'Banfield's/Trudgeon's dwelling house and mills'

Old Bar Mill, by William J. Boase Smith, with Symon's/Harvey's yard in the background, *c.*1885. Children play and swim amongst the vessels in the creek. (Falmouth Art Gallery.)

and 'Netherton's/Jessop's mills'. In the latter case the wording included 'a good sum laid out in building £30', and in 1760 'a good sum laid out in building £30' was also applied to the earlier Banfield lease. The leases were renewed in 1766, but this time to Richard Bluett, possibly the son of the earlier Richard. He is recorded as a shipbuilder in *Bailey's Western and Midland Directory* of 1783. Susan E. Gay stated that Richard Bluett 'of Barr, near Falmouth' was a manufacturer of blocks and masts at the Bar, and that he died in 1791 while returning from a visit to Holcombe, which was a family seat in South Devon. He had nine children (his wife, Sarah, gave birth to eleven), some of the sons achieving high ranks in the army and navy. It is obvious that the Bluetts were not millers themselves, but employed, or sub-let to, professional millers. Towards the end of the Arwenack steward's lease book a note states that in August 1792 the Bar properties were held by Mrs Sarah Bluett; thereafter the book is silent. Curiously, in 1799 the *Universal British Directory* lists Richard Bluett as a shipbuilder. Perhaps his widow wanted his name perpetuated in the company title. According to Gay, one of the sons was called Richard, but he was said to be a Post Captain in the Royal Navy. This conundrum is resolved within the chapter on the Bar shipbuilders.

Low water at the Bar, *c.*1890. The mill is in the centre, fronted by Harvey's yard with vessels on the beach. Lean's jetty and the Manor Yard are to the right, with the Dock Inn behind the trees. To the left are Burt's yard and Lean's outer yard, with the railway sheds and dock grain store above and left. (RCPS.)

DECLINE

There is no record of the working life, decline and removal of the small Banfield/ Trudgeon mill: it is clearly depicted on the 1773 Falmouth map, but not included on Thomas's map of 1827. The building and tide sluice aperture can just be seen on Allen's view of 1831. It may have been demolished by the time the print was published. This was the fate of many small mills in the following century. Large steam-powered mills, driving multiple sets of stones, were built in a number of Cornish towns, including Truro, and from the 1830s the highly efficient roller-milling process was brought into the country. Cheap imported flour was another factor: an advertisement in the *West Briton* on 11 May 1812 offered for sale the surplus from a cargo of 3,000 barrels of American flour 'perfectly sound and of superior quality' which had been imported on the ship *Archimedes* for the Committee of Truro Householders.

Shipbuilder Robert Symons of Bar Mill (now the name for Netherton's mill) is recorded in *Pigot's Directory* of 1823, although Robert had drowned in the harbour in October 1821. Some of the family may have migrated across the water from the Little Falmouth yard, where the Symons had been building and repairing ships, including packet ships, from the mid-eighteenth century. Previously that yard had been the site of 'Lobb's Pilchard Palace', famous for processing and exporting pilchards as far as Naples and Venice. The pervading smell of fish may have somewhat abated by the time the residing landowners, the Trefusis family, were developing the adjacent hamlet of Flushing as a base for the packet ships and accommodation for crews, captains and passengers. At some time

Bar Mill and tidal pool, *c.*1897. The mill is in the last stages of disintegration. The sluice apertures are clearly seen in this low-tide view, as is the collapsing dam wall on the left. (RCPS.)

Bar Mill, *c.*1897. Some interesting features of the construction of the building and dam can be seen in this otherwise sad picture. A schooner lies high and dry in Lean's outer yard beyond. (RCPS.)

before 1823 Francis Symons had taken over the whole of the Bar area previously leased to the Bluetts. In 1841 he was still responsible for paying the tithes for the area, defined in the apportionment book as just over 11 acres. This information is somewhat at odds with the 1848 Wodehouse Estate conveyance list of lessees, which gives Catherine Griffin as leasing that whole area, including the shipwrights' yards, mill and Bar House, including the bath house and baths at the quay. (See below.) Unfortunately nothing else is known of this lady, apart from that she was the mother of Lieutenant Griffin, believed to be a packet ship commander. Bar Mill was then still being worked: the 1841 census lists James Brimacombe as miller, and he re-appears in the *Post Office Directory* for 1856. The last documentary evidence for this mill as a going concern is, ironically, on a proposal plan for the development of Falmouth Docks: beside the building on Netherton's great dam are the simple words 'Flour Mills'.

Perhaps Richard, a relation of James Brimacombe, had the future in mind in *his* chosen occupation: the directories list him as 'Beer Retailer and Ginger Beer Maker, Bar'. Shipbuilder Francis Symons was also diversifying: in April 1831 he was advertising that his public baths would be opening in May, with hot, cold, vapour, medicated and salt water baths:

> Invalids and others may be accommodated in lodgings at the house of Mr Symons, close to the above baths …. a pleasant walk from the town, in the most delightful part of the neighbourhood…

In June he added that bathing machines would be placed on the beach in a short time. One wonders what Mrs Symons thought of these disruptive entrepreneurial efforts, as the *Falmouth Packet Births* column the previous year recorded that on 30 June, at Bar House, she gave birth to a son.

It is not known when Symons gave up the mill and shipyard. Perhaps he saw the writing on the wall and moved out of Bar House, for the 'most delightful part of the neighbourhood' was not to remain so. From the 1860s, as spoil from the building of the docks and railway began to engulf the Bar pools, the mill building gradually disintegrated, a process graphically depicted by contemporary artists and photographers. Harveys of Hayle took over the Symons shipyard on the outer Bar in 1887; the lease issued by the Kimberley Estate also included what was left of the tide mill building. A further lease of 1906 stated that, because of necessary adjacent works by the docks company, Harveys could remove the remains of the Bar Mill and deposit them on some convenient part of their land. In other words, dump them in what was left of the mill pool. There is evidence that this had already been achieved: the building is not shown on Lake's town map of 1900. It had certainly disappeared by the time of the survey for the 1908 large-scale Ordnance Survey map.

THREE

SHIPWRIGHTS AND SAILORS

HARBOUR HAPPENINGS

A population census in 1801 gives the number of males in Falmouth parish as 1,963; they were far out-numbered by 2,886 females. There were also about 500 sailors and soldiers, many of the latter garrisoning Pendennis Castle. The reason for the male/female imbalance is unclear, although the war against Napoleon is an obvious factor. Many local men, with their knowledge of the sea, may have sought a paid berth on a ship of the Royal Navy, or, if not so inclined, would have been eagerly sought by the press-gangs which were active along the coast. Any lack of male workers would not have affected the economy of Falmouth. Women did a variety of jobs just as well as men; on the land, in the pilchard cellars, or perhaps the shipbuilding industry as sail-makers and the like. In a transit port such as Falmouth, many were employed as seamstresses, bakers, cooks and in the boarding houses and inns. Some women provided other needs for sailors when the fleet arrived: the Rabelaisian life of the town is glimpsed in a painting by J. M. W. Turner, who visited Cornwall in around 1811. In a view of the harbour and Pendennis from The Beacon, overlooking the town, he depicts in the foreground a somewhat bawdy scene reminiscent of William Hogarth. A number of 'Jolly Jack Tars' from the fleet anchored below have the company of four girls from the town. One gazes at a fiddle player, her upset linen basket forgotten, others assist the sailors with bottles of liquor. All seem to be 'three sheets to the wind', as two empty kegs plummet down the hill towards the town below.

In 1819, William Penaluna provided a vivid picture of the haven at the peak of England's naval might under sail in the years following Trafalgar:

In the winter of 1805, the Hon. Adml. Cornwallis sailed into this harbour several times, at low water, with five or six sail of heavy three-deckers and a scanty wind. In all southerly winds verging from the east to west, within twenty points of the compass, the largest ships of the British navy can enter Carrig Roads, through the deep channel, at any time of the

J M. W. Turner's view of Falmouth from The Beacon, *c.*1811. (Cornwall Centre.)

tide, even at dead low water, during the lowest springs. In the beginning of the year 1815, a fleet of 350 vessels, including ships of war, and merchantmen of great burden, took shelter in this harbour, and rode out several severe gales, without sustaining any damage. The entrance, which is about one mile in width, is easy of access, that the packets, without any assistance, can run in at all times, without any apprehension of danger. The free ingress and egress at any time obtainable, and the ease at which the ocean is gained from this harbour, render it superior to any other in the kingdom, for the purpose of transatlantic navigation.

At times Falmouth had been used as a naval victualling base and it was thought that eventually it could become the major West Country base for the fleet, however it must be said that not all in power viewed the haven in such glowing terms. Some naval commanders saw disadvantages such as shoals in the anchorage and the length of an overland supply route. Others remembered the night in January 1814, when the *Queen* transport ship's anchor cables parted in a storm and she was driven ashore and quickly broke up on Trefusis Point. She had been bringing back home injured and sick soldiers of Wellington's army, plus many women, children and French officer prisoners. Estimates of the number of fatalities vary. However, of a compliment of about 350 passengers and crew, 100 men and four (or seven) women reached the shore alive. A memorial to this tragic event, set up by local people at the time, can still be seen in Mylor churchyard. Intense lobbying by Plymouth also helped to guarantee that that great naval base continued to dominate the South West.

Falmouth Harbour is sheltered from severe weather from the more westerly points of the compass but open to the south and east. The vulnerability of the harbour in

HMS *Ganges*, the boys' training ship, based in the Carrick Roads from 1865 to 1899, seen here with other 'square-riggers' in the Inner Harbour with a quay punt alongside. *Ganges* was built of teak in Bombay in 1821. She saw little active service but represents the fleets of men-of-war which often graced the waters of Falmouth Haven. (RCPS.)

southerly gales was highlighted in the local newspaper *The West Briton* of 11 January 1828. It concerned the unlucky brig *Larch*, which was at first incorrectly reported as *Sarah*, there only being the alteration of two letters to cause the confusion. The report illustrates that the Cornish were more likely to risk their own lives to save mariners rather than indulging in deliberate 'wrecking'. It also describes the ingenious use of a large barrel as an early 'Breeches Bouy', the wonderful life-saving device which was being perfected at the time by Henry Trengrouse of Helston. William Broad later received the Royal National Lifeboat Institutes' Gold Medal for assisting in the rescue of the eleven souls on board.

On Monday last, it blew a tremendous gale from the South East, which continued without intermission during the whole of the day. About noon, the brig *Sarah*, of 150 tons burthen, Thomas Collingwood, master, from Newfoundland for Poole, with a cargo of fish, oil and lumber, sought shelter from the storm by running into Falmouth Harbour. The state of the weather prevented any of the pilot boats keeping the sea, and she consequently entered without the usual assistance, and brought up too near the shore. After dragging her anchor for some time, by 3 o'clock in the afternoon she drifted close to the rocks on the Trefusis side of the harbour, and hoisted a signal of distress. Mr Broad, agent for Lloyd's at the port, immediately put off in a six-oared gig, and was followed by one of his pilots; with difficulty they got on board, but all their efforts to free her from her perilous situation were ineffectual, as she drifted on the rocks close to the new Quay pier. As the gale continued with unabated fury and the night was falling in, the lives of those on board were placed in jeopardy. At the suggestion of Capt. Sutton of H.M. packet Stanmer, the inhabitants of Flushing made a good light with furze and tar barrels on an adjacent hill, which was of great advantage; the masts of the brig were necessarily cut away, and a cable being conveyed on shore, the crew, with a gentleman and his two daughters, passengers, were got safely to land in an empty cask which was slung and traversed on the cable. The vessel fortunately held together until the gale abated; the cargo is being discharged and the hull will be got off in the course of the coming spring tides. – The brig was 21 days on her passage, which was a most boisterous one, and during which all the crew, but the master, were frost bitten, so as to be unable to render effective assistance. Great praise is due to the inhabitants of Flushing for their prompt and active assistance afforded in saving the crew, and for the sympathy manifested in affording them every comfort their distressed situation required, on their being got on shore.

At the end of that month Falmouth merchant William Broad advertised the auction of the cargo of *Larch*. The ship's manifest vividly brings to mind scenes of oilskinned cod fishermen fighting wind, waves and weather in frail dories on the Grand Banks and fur-clad trappers and lumberjacks working deep in the pine forests of a frozen northern wilderness.

An advertisement for the sale of *Larch* appeared in the *Falmouth Packet* in July 1829. She was of 150 tons register and carried about 200 tons, having been built only eighteen months. Her hull was described as exceedingly handsome, with a figurehead. The brig was bought by Mayn & Co. and appeared in *Lloyd's Register* of 1831 under that ownership; described as of 149 tons and Newfoundland built. However, a second local disaster soon befell *Larch*, the circumstances of which are unknown. On 5 February 1831, the *Falmouth Packet* advertised the auction of her hull, 'lately stranded and broken up,' together with masts, rigging and sails, some of which had never been used. The broker was Mr Corfield of Penryn.

A disruptive gale occurred in February 1838 and was described in the journal of twenty-year-old Robert Barclay Fox, of the family of Quaker shipping agents and merchants in Falmouth. It proves that sudden severe weather is not a new phenomenon:

15th. A most terrible night was followed by an equally tempestuous day. Wind S.E. Took a run before breakfast, but found it no joke to make head against the storm. The snow driving in your face like a simoom and stinging like hail, and lying on the ground in vast drifts to the depth of one and two feet. Found at the office that a packet had driven ashore at Trefusis Pt. and in the intervals, when the snow became a little less thick, we could make her out lying on the rocks on her beam ends, with top-gallant masts and all the yards set. We could also see that the *Asia*, a Dutch East Indiaman of 1,100 tons, had driven awfully near the point….. I could make out the packet clearly. She proved to be the *Ranger*, Lt.. Turner, in a most awful plight. Trudged up to Boyer's Cellars to look at the devastation along the shore: a sloop belonging to F. Symons, knocking to pieces at Market Strand, having carried away a corner of the *King's Arms*; another at Green Bank, hammering away at the pier in which she had bored a great cavity, was going to destruction as fast as possible; another was run ashore at Boyer's. We blocked up the doorway with bales of wool. The old brig was rolling it out on two anchors, but the Dutch galliot at Symons's yard was blown clean over, her bulwarks, cross-trees, and a little bit of deck were just visible above the waves.

Oil, Skins, Plank, Staves, &c.

AN AUCTION will be held at the Cellars on the North Quay, *Falmouth*, by J. ELLIS, on THURSDAY the 7th of February next, by Eleven o'Clock in the Forenoon, for SELLING the

CARGO

Of the Brig Larch, from Newfoundland lately Stranded in this Port, comprising

44 Hogsheads and Barrels of Train Cod Oil and Dregs or Pitchings,
12 Hogsheads and Barrels of Cod Blubber.
 7   ditto   ditto   Dog Fish Oil.
15   ditto   ditto   Seal   ditto.
 9   ditto   ditto   Caplin.
 1 Box Dried Cod and Caplin.
 2 Casks pickled Cod Fish.
 1 Hogshead and 1 Bundle of Furs, viz.
78 Beavers.
 1 Silver Fox.
 1 Patch ditto.
15 Yellow ditto.
 5 White ditto.
56 Martin Skins.
17 Musk Rat ditto.
 4 lbs. of Beaver prides.
2½ Mille of Fir Staves.
354 Pine Plank of various dimensions.
36 Juniper Plank.
About 3 dozen small Spars and Poles.
 9 Bags of Nails.
300 empty Bread bags.
For viewing or further particulars, apply to the Broker, or to

W. Broad and Sons,

Merchants.

January 31, 1828.

Right: Notice in the *West Briton* newspaper, 2 February 1828.

Below: Merchant vessels, plus an elegant steam yacht, huddle close to the town on a dismal but calm morning, possibly after seeking shelter during the 'great blizzard' of 1891. (RCPS.)

The first RNLI lifeboat for Falmouth, the *Gloucester*, was installed in a boathouse at the docks in 1867. Although early craft were only propelled by oar and sail, many heroic rescues were undertaken. But it was not until the development of powerful harbour steam tugs and, from 1931, a motor-driven lifeboat, that there were the means to tow disabled vessels away from the treacherous coast. In the centuries of sail disasters such as those highlighted above, danger had to be an acceptable part of going to sea.

Regarding contemporary adverse comments about shoals in the harbour; tidal scouring movements in the Fal have meant that little artificial dredging was necessary over recent centuries to keep the main navigation channel open to Truro. Nevertheless, great care has to be taken to keep to the narrow channel through the mudbanks in the upper reaches. When the Falmouth docks were under construction from 1861 the old Bar Point and shoals had to be removed by steam-dredgers to allow deep-drafted vessels to reach the wharves and dry docks. Prior to the invention of such mechanical means, little could be done to remove shoals which might have caused problems to vessels in the Inner Harbour and Penryn River; not that earlier attempts *were not* made. In 1796 Sir John Wodehouse, who with Lord De Dunstanville was 'Lord of the soil of the Inner Harbour', instructed James Moor of Falmouth to employ and oversee for twelve months Mylor mariners Edmond Harvey, Richard Rundle and Richard Rickeard, to diligently employ themselves 'unless prevented by strong and tempestuous wind and weather', to take up sand, dirt and other rubbish out of the harbour, as directed by James Moor. They were loaned the barge *Arwenack* and were to 'preserve and take care of the said barge, her sails, rigging, tackle, apparel, boat and furniture'. They were each to be paid 18 shillings monthly and were to account to Moor for the sale of sand and so on to farmers (seaweed, sand and shells were valued land fertilizers). They were given an incentive to work, as farmers were expected to give them a shilling a barge load for drink! However, it is not likely that substantial changes were made to harbour depths from this contract.

About forty years later the harbour communities may have had the first intimation that the Falmouth-based Post Office packet ships, which had become a vital part of the commercial and social life of the port, might be removed to Plymouth or Southampton. This may have prompted Lords Wodehouse and De Dunstanville to employ Henry Habberley Price to make the first detailed survey of the Inner Harbour. A series of boreholes found many feet of sand and shell towards Bar Point, with no rocky ground to interfere with proposed dredging. The packet anchorage, 9 acres of water between Green Bank and Flushing, had depths at low water of 10-14ft (3-4m). The moorings consisted of five sets of ground chains of 2.5in (6.25cm) iron, 45-50 fathoms in length, apparently only sufficient for seven vessels, although twenty-six were on the station. This number was less than before because steam-boats were now used on the Mediterranean station. Nothing seems to have been done following this survey, although the subject of dredging to accommodate larger vessels was obviously discussed and various remedies suggested, such as that witnessed by Robert Barclay Fox in August 1838:

> Joined the Harbour Committee at the Bar to see Lieut. Green's wind-sail dredging apparatus applied to the mud in the harbour. As I sagely foretold it proved but an airy scheme and ended in flatulence.

In spite of intense lobbying by the Foxs and their allies in the town, which included discussions for the Cornwall Railway to connect Falmouth to London for the benefit of packet passengers and the mail, the packet station was removed from Falmouth by 1850.

In 1814 Lysons stated that Falmouth's trade was suffering because of the war (with France) but gives a list of imports which were landed during more prosperous times. The list includes tobacco, wood, wheat and Indian corn (maize) from North America; fruit, wine, brandy, wool and salt from Spain and Portugal; cheese, butter and grain from Holland; shipbuilding supplies from Northern Europe and Russia; hides, sugar, cotton and wool from South America; grain, flour, fruit, salt, wine and brandy from France; coal, iron, earthen-ware, and salt from Wales and Liverpool. Tin and pilchards continued to be the main exports to a number of countries; others included copper, iron, cotton and woollen goods. There was regular passage of ships from London and Bristol, bringing in large supplies of groceries, the London ships (usually in convoy) returning to the capital with tin. As trade increased through the centuries, some Falmouth merchants began to purchase, or have shares in, their own ships. There were plenty of second-hand merchantmen available: one example of this came in an advertisement in the *Falmouth Packet* for July 1829, which offered for auction the 170-ton brig *Edward,* the 190-ton schooner *Bideford* and the 96-ton schooner *John*. The vessels lay in Falmouth and were 'peculiarly adapted for the coal, coasting and foreign trade'.

As early as 1668 there were enough expert shipwrights, mast makers and riggers in the locality for the town to celebrate the launch of its first ship, *The Falmouth Frigatt*, referred to previously. Unfortunately the location of the yard is unknown, but the Bar is a possibility. By the early eighteenth century a shipbuilding infrastructure was well established in the town, a situation corroborated by the leasing in 1737 of the old ornamental avenue within the manor grounds to be turned into a rope walk. The long, perfectly straight Arwenack Avenue still exists. Small fishing boats had been built around the shores and creeks for centuries, and some still are. The oyster-dredging fleet, the larger versions once mainly consisting of craft from Porthleven and elsewhere, were developed by local shipwrights as shallow-draughted, cutter-rigged versions of the quay punts, into the distinctive 'Falmouth working boats' of today. However, as mercantile trade increased during the nineteenth century, there was a need for a large fleet of small merchantmen, and yards expanded to satisfy the demand. Before their trade was taken away by an improved road system and motor vehicles, throughout the Victorian era hundreds of small brigantines, barges, schooners and ketches were to be seen around the British coast, some travelling much further afield.

The major requirement for building wooden ships is, of course, good timber. At one time local landowners seemed keen to profit from their estate timber by offering it for auction in local newspapers. For instance – 246 mature oak trees, complete with their tops and bark, from an estate at Menheniot, were advertised for auction in the *Falmouth Packet* in January 1830. The timber was said to be of great length and large dimensions, well adapted for navy purposes, such as keelsons, plank, logs and so on. The trees were within four miles of Tideford River, from whence they could be shipped to any part of the kingdom. However, local timber would have provided only a small amount of that which was required for so many uses apart from shipbuilding. Dozens of tin and copper mines

Harbour scene, *c*.1900. The heavily laden vessel on the left is the 158-ton brigantine *Fredericke*, possibly carrying Baltic timber. She was built and registered at Papenburg, North Germany in 1886 and wrecked in 1904. (RCPS.)

used massive timbers for supporting construction work and shoring underground. Smaller-sized timber had 101 different uses, from barrel making to house building.

Dr J.A.C. Whetter, whose books and research papers are required reading for any study of the history of Falmouth, has provided valuable statistics on the very considerable importation of timber from Scandinavia from the late seventeenth century onwards. One of the most notable features of the 1773 map of Falmouth is the artist's representation of baulks of timber, stacked on the road side in front of the manor house, on the outer Bar, and floating for preservation and seasoning in the tidal pools. Imported pine logs for masts and spars were seasoned in salt water, because the process allowed the sap to die back without drying out the timber's resins: this allowed the wood to remain supple and capable of bending, rather than breaking under the weight of wind and sails. Timber ponds also existed elsewhere on the Fal, such as at Restronguet Creek, Penryn and Truro. Timber ships anchoring in the Inner Harbour near the Bar could discharge their cargo overboard, which might then be rafted into the Bar pools for storage until required by shipyards or elsewhere. Agents and dealers gathered on the waterfront at the arrival of a ship, or responded to an advertisement in the local paper, such as in October 1830, when twenty-four 'capitol' black spruce spars, from 40-50ft (12m-15m) in length, were auctioned in lots near the Bar. By the 1860s the pools were described on maps as timber ponds rather than mill pools. The timber was conveniently place for any shipwrights who had established themselves on the Bar. The 1773 map maker included representations of a number of small craft and larger ships within the area, indicating that there was already a yard here.

A beautiful and accurate model of an early quay punt, possibly *Pride of the Port*, whereabouts unknown. (Photo RCPS.)

Two elegant quay punts wait for the tide to lift them off after hull-cleaning on Grove Place Beach. (RCPS.)

QUAY PUNTS

As world-wide trade increased throughout the reign of Victoria, even greater numbers of merchant ships were sailing into Falmouth. The shipping returns for the port in 1894 list about 1,200 craft calling, although not all necessarily stopping, of which far less than half were English; the majority of the rest being Scandinavian, German and Italian. Consequently a type of small sailing boat known as a quay punt had replaced earlier rowed or lug-rigged boats that tended ships while anchored in the Bay or Carrick Roads. Quay punt skippers, usually single-handed, took their boats far out to sea in the same quest for incoming ships as the pilot cutters, to obtain permission from Masters to provide services for them while in port. They then acted as go-betweens twixt ship and shore, carrying provisions, agents and officers, or passing messages. There is an illustration of a Trethowan quay punt in the 1888 edition of Dixon Kemp's *Manual of Yacht and Boat Sailing*, where they are described thus:

> These boats bear a very close resemblance to those of Itchen Ferry and are wonderfully handy and seaworthy. Boys – some as young as ten years – constantly knock them about the harbour single-handed, whilst it is the event of every day and night for a man to go 'seeking' in them alone, in all weathers, to the Lizard and even beyond, getting away as far as forty miles from harbour, and they remain at sea sometimes for a day or two. These boats vary in size from 20ft to 30ft over all, and from 7ft to 10ft beam, drawing from 3ft to 6ft of water; they are decked in to about two-fifths of their length from the stem; they have waterways 1ft wide, and coamings, and all have square sterns – no counters. Freeboard, 2ft 6in to 3ft. The rig is uniform also, viz., gaff mainsail with boom, jib-headed mizen, and foresail set on a short iron bumpkin – simplicity itself – and, with patent blocks everywhere, and small ropes, everything is well within the strength of an ordinary man.

The professional quay puntsmen, when not perhaps waiting off the Lizard to be first to 'speak', and therefore be informally contracted to incoming ships, were based on Custom House Quay. Sometimes, as they fruitlessly rolled around for several days far out at sea in the hope of sighting an incoming sail, some may have yearned for a job ashore. But on other occasions, with a steady flow of windjammers 'calling for orders', life was good, and could be lucrative. Adverse weather could be a blessing in disguise, such as in April 1895, when the *Falmouth Packet* reported that seventeen merchant steamers, thirty large full-rigged ships, twenty-five sail of the French fishing fleet, Lowestoft smacks and smaller craft were sheltering in the harbour. As the puntsmen rested in their shelter by the 'King's Pipe' on the quay (the incinerator where contraband tobacco was burnt), the conversation might drift to the subject of the summer's racing, and to whether or not the latest punt to come off the blocks would be good enough to beat so and so's boat. Traditionally, half models, to a shape agreed between customer and builder, were made before work commenced on constructing the hull. However, as races became ever-more competitive, professionally designed plans began to be used; winning races meant further orders!

After diligent research, over 150 Falmouth-built quay punts have now been recorded on the Bartlett Library database. About thirty-two are known to have been working boats, the

R.S. Burt's *Olive*, built in 1913, sails past other quay punts moored off the waterfront in May 1924. (NMM Greenwich.)

majority as leisure day-boats or small cruising yachts. Not many achieved the fame of R.S. Burt's *Curlew* or *I.C.U.*, discussed later, and apart from some beautiful half-models, the shipwrights left few records of their output. Small working craft were built to the order of watermen, fishermen or quay puntsmen, and used until they were irreparably wrecked or rotted away, unless they were reprieved and restored, sometimes at considerable expense, by a yachting enthusiast. The history of *Wild Duck* seems to have taken this course: built by Burt in 1894 for puntsmen William and Reginald Tonkin, in about 1920 she was sold and converted to a yacht for G. Romney Fox, possibly being lengthened from 28 to 32 ft., (8.5 to 9.7m). At least two further owners were involved in keeping her going for the next 50 years, and she was being refitted in 1972. At about that time she was photographed afloat on the River Hamble. She still exists as a derelict shell, ashore at a Fal boatyard, a suitable candidate for restoration. Another boat built for the Tonkin family, this time for Alfred, was *Olive*, possibly built by Burt in 1913. By then there may have been less work out at sea for the puntsmen, or Alfred needed a less arduous occupation, for *Olive* was used primarily for charter leisure trips around Falmouth.

Of the multifarious duties of the quay punts, the work of 'The *Fat Boat*' of St Mawes stands out. This was described by Jimmy Morrison in the booklet *Living History Under Sail* produced by the Falmouth Working Boats Association in 1982:

> The Fat Boat's function was to take off for sale ashore the big accumulation of fat from all the cooking that had been done on the voyage. A sort of cook's perk it was. With hundreds

of sailing ships calling here, there was a hell of accumulation of surplus fat coming in and the Fat Boat used to collect it, and sell it, boiled up, to the poorer people at a penny a pound or cheaper…

The *Fat Boat*, crewed by two young men, Bill Weatherby of Flushing and Brian Pascoe, came to a tragic end in 1904 in a race with *I.C.U.* to a ship off the Lizard. 'The *Fat Boat* went into one wave solid, filled up and they never seen her again. The *I.C.U.* came up to the position, but there was not a trace.'

PILOT CUTTERS

In 1809 Henry Vincent of St Mawes became the first local pilot to be licensed by Trinity House. Thereafter the family, plus various shareholders, owned a number of cutters for much of the nineteenth century. The list includes several named *Vincent* and two *Harriet*. Other familes in St Mawes and Falmouth had boats built and produced several generations of sons to sail them. Well-known names include Andrew, Bickford, Collins, Dash, Fittock, Green and Lowry.

Although merchant ships today have sophisticated navigation equipment, professional pilots are still often required to guide them safely into port. Their employment was vital in the days of sail when local knowledge of winds, tides and unmarked shoals could provide safe passage for vessels arriving in unknown waters. Over several centuries a great variety of vessels had the arrangement of sails known as cutter-rig. Basically that means one main mast, with a top mast above it, carrying a 'fore and aft' main and topsail. Traditionally the mainsail was held up by a spar called a gaff. A triangular sail was set on the forestay between bow and mast, plus two or more set on a long bow-sprit, a horizontal spar in front of the bow. Well-designed long-keeled boats with this rig, being sea–worthy, fast, and easy to handle, were adopted by pilots at home and abroad. Unlike Bristol Channel cutters, a number of which are still sailed as yachts (and similar versions being built), no Falmouth boats have survived, therefore information about them must be gleaned from records and photographs. Although a few were built along the coast at Plymouth, Mevagissey and possibly Porthleven, where James Sandry received orders from South Wales pilots, most Falmouth cutters were locally produced.

In the mid-1840s the average length from bow to counter was about 48ft (14.60m), but within a decade Falmouth pilots were demanding craft of 60ft (18m) and over. Accommodation consisted perhaps of a galley, saloon and bunks for up to four or more pilots and apprentices, plus perhaps two boatmen. That number was required because several ships might arrive within hours: pilots took turns to board ships to pass on sailing instructions or take them into the port. Decks were flush between raised bulwarks up to a metre in height. Access below was via a hatch and companionway in the steering well at the stern; steering was by tiller. Unless the sea was very calm, the pilots' punt, a dinghy up to about 4m in length, was used to take a pilot across to the ship he was attending. It was normally kept on deck blocks abaft the mast. A tackle may have been used to swing it out-board and retrieve it. A section of bulwark could be removed to assist this.

Pilot cutter No.6, *Arrow*, built by John Trethowan in 1863. Her massive but elegant 35-ton hull lies on Grove Place Beach for cleaning, painting or re-caulking. The Submarine Pier and the Bar are in the background. There is another cutter immediately behind her, the reason for the apparent excessive amount of rigging. (NMM Greenwich.)

The most distinctive feature of the Falmouth boats (according to available photographs) was that the mainsail was loose-footed, that is, there was no boom holding the lower edge of the sail. Instead, a powerful main sheet tackle was hooked between the clew of the sail and a 'horse' or iron bar on the counter in similar fashion to a Thames bawley. The sail was in two separate sections: when heavy weather was expected, the larger upper part attached to the gaff would be set at a lowish height on the mast, and could also be reefed. In fine weather, and for racing, a 'bonnet', an extra strip of sail, possibly up to 2m in width, was laced onto the foot of the sail. With the gaff raised higher; a topsail could then be set if required. This seemingly primitive and awkward method of sail reduction or addition was common on square-rigged ships up until the mid-seventeenth century when reefing points were reinvented. It has also been used on small sprit-sails and schooner foresails.

The heyday of the sailing cutters was in the mid-nineteenth century, when perhaps up to 200 ships a month might be expected to appear over the horizon and the boats raced each other out into the Western Approaches to obtain the right to escort vessels into the port, or at least obtain a fee for passing messages from owners or agents. All pilots had to undertake seven-year apprenticeships, two of those years 'deep water' sailing in square-rigged ships. First or second class certificates were issued by Trinity House, some men going on to be Channel pilots, taking vessels to other British, or perhaps

Arrow, with full mainsail set, including the bonnet, *c.*1900. The neat line of lacings or ties are clearly seen. (RCPS.)

Pilot cutter No.8, *Vincent*, built in 1852 at Stonehouse, Plymouth for William Vincent of St Mawes, and at 21m one of the longest of the cutter fleet. Her long-time owner retired in 1894 but she remained as a pilot boat with the Association and was last recorded, then seventy years old, under the private ownership of Michael Edwards of Porhan Street, Falmouth. Here she carries the mainsail of *Harriet* which may have been de-commissioned. Note the lack of bonnet resulting in an incredibly long mainsheet tackle. Note also the side-cloths protecting the helmsman and the stowed boarding punt. (RCPS.)

Continental ports. As the century progressed there was a gradual decline in work for all pilots. Merchant ships became larger but fewer in number. Many were now driven by powerful steam engines and independent of contrary winds. Communications were also improving: ships arriving in the Western Approaches normally passed close to the Lizard, the most southern point of Britain, where there was a lighthouse and coastguard station. After pressure from shipping agents G.C. Fox & Co. in 1872, the Post Office laid an overland telegraph cable to the Lizard. Fox & Co., later joined by William Broad & Co., then developed a signal station on nearby Bass Point, installing telegraph transmitters and receivers. They then advertised that passing vessels should contact the station, in the early days perhaps by semaphore or lamp, so that their passing could be reported to owners. Agents in Falmouth then sent out sealed orders via the pilots. Messages could also now be sent directly to Lloyds of London for their daily shipping list. In late 1872 Bass Point became the terminal of the submarine telegraph cable from Bilbao, bringing important shipping news directly from northern Spain. Twentieth-century technology later came to the Lizard with Marconi's development of radio: eventually vessels with the new equipment could communicate directly between ship and shore.

In 1887, individual earnings for the sixty or more pilots based in St Mawes and Falmouth were still diminishing. Therefore the decision was made to amalgamate and form the Falmouth District Pilot Boat Association, under the auspices of Trinity House. Of the twelve existing boats, five were sold off to save on upkeep, leaving, under 'managing owners', *Andrews* (F. Andrew); *Antelope* (S. Collins); *Arrow* (W.J. Lowry); *Condor* (J.J. Vincent); *Harriet* (M. Richards); *Richard Green* (C. Andrew) and *Vincent* (W. Vincent). A daily rota was organised for groups of pilots to share work on the seven boats which often operated round the clock. Four or more pilots might be aboard each boat, taking turns in boarding vessels to bring them into port or merely passing messages. Various fees were paid for pilotage, depending on distance, in or out of the harbour and size of vessel. Some knowledge of the daily life of the sailing cutter pilots may be gathered, albeit towards the end of their era, from the 1907 logbook of *Condor*, cutter No.12. This 18m, 32-ton boat was built by Trethowan at Little Falmouth in 1874 for J.J. Vincent of St Mawes. He remained as managing owner under the Association but by 1907 the Master was Hugh Andrew. By 1913 *Condor* had been sold to the locally well-known Walter Morrison for use as a yacht. She then passed through several hands before being abandoned in the Percuil River. In July 1942, a Custom and Excise notice to the owner regarding the certificate of registry stated that she had been reported broken up.

In 1887 the cutters' cruising areas had been allocated thus – two to cruise within twenty miles of the Lizard, one stationed at the Lizard, one to cruise between Lizard and the Manacles, one between the Manacles and the Dodman headland to the east, one on harbour duties and another for emergencies. It is likely that by 1907 this number of locations had already been reduced. *Condor's* beat was in the Lizard/Manacles vicinity. Pilots recorded in the boats' logbook the position, type, name and nationality of every vessel taken charge of, boarded, or spoken to. The weather, wind direction and strength was recorded every four hours. The pilots at that time attached to *Condor* were H. Green, E. Hodge, C. Jenkin, C. Fittock, J. Sawle, F. Andrew and F. Watts with Hugh Andrew, Master. However, other groups of pilots also used the boat at times. Work for the pilots was so slack that several days might go by with no ships recorded; those that did appear were usually calling for their shipping orders. These were already on board the pilot boats, the agents in Falmouth having previous notification of the ship's arrival off the Lizard. Typical entries in the logbook were:

Friday 7th June 1907

1am Wind W3 Overcast.	St Anthony SW by N, 6 miles. Boarded German S/S (Steamship) *Marionfels* from Antwerp. F. Andrew, Pilot.	
5am Wind WSW4	Boarded English ship *Endora* from Australia for orders. C. Fittock, Pilot.	
8 am "	Boarded Italian Barque *N.S. del Rosana* (?) from Montevideo for orders. H. Andrew, Pilot.	
11am "	Lizard N by E, 4 miles.	
Noon "	Boarded Russian Barque *Woolf* from Buenos Ayres for orders. H. Green, Pilot.	
4pm "	Lizard NNE, 4 miles. Boarded Norway Sch (Schooner) *Haave* from Rio Grande for orders. E. Hodge, Pilot.	
Midnight	In the harbour for pilots.	

Throughout the Victorian era, in company with servicing boats such as gigs and later quay punts, the cutters and their crews were an important link between the town and visiting vessels entering the harbour, bringing financial benefits in the form of shipyard employment and the sale of provisions. They were justifiably appreciated, particularly when on show at the regattas. The Falmouth town Regatta was held around August each year. In 1853 the report in the *Royal Cornwall Gazette* lists only a few competing yachts compared to the classes for the small traditional sailing boats, (many skippered by shipwrights), fishing luggers and oyster-dredging boats. According to the reporter's unedited and excited write-up, the cutters, thirteen in all, certainly made the best show, competing on two rounds of a course across Falmouth Bay. The race began off Flushing Quay:

> First on their slipping their bouys, up going the jibs, and steadily moving down the Inner Harbour, showing first-rate seamanship, and from such a crowd of sail being in such proximity, presented as beautiful a spectacle as ever a regatta produced. In truth the whole course of these fine vessels was marked with extreme interest, most of them being new, and one, of the largest tonnage allowed by the Trinity Board….. The view at this time was a most exciting one, and would well tempt the lovers of yacht sailing in any part of the kingdom….

J.Vincent's *Vincent* was the eventual winner, with E. Chard's *Victoria* a close second, after a topsail halyard carried away, and N.Vincent in *Harriet*, third.These particular craft were still competing twenty years later, either in the Royal Cornwall Yacht Club or Town and Quay regattas.

The dangers of the sea were always present. Even skilled mariners such as pilots could make mistakes and get into difficulties. One even put the ship he was piloting aground on the familiar Black Rock at the harbour entrance. Some pilot boats and crews were lost at sea. One incident which fortunately did not lead to loss of life was reported in the *Falmouth and Penryn Weekly Times* in December 1892.

ACCIDENT TO FALMOUTH PILOTS – No.1 pilot cutter, Falmouth, was off the Lizard on Thursday morning and about eight o'clock the boat put off, in order that T.H. Coward, pilot, and E. Lowry and William Andrew might board the Swedish barque *Livingstone*, from River Plate to Falmouth, for orders. When the boat got alongside, the sea curled under the vessel's quarter, causing the boat to run ahead on the top of the wave. It then turned over, and the three men were thrown into the water. Fortunately, Mr Coward grasped the bottom rung of the ladder hanging over the ship's side; another caught hold of a rope hanging over, whilst the third slipped his arm through a chain plate. Some of the crew sprang over and came to their rescue, and all were saved. They were in an exhausted condition, the sea being very rough. The cutter's boat was afterwards picked up by the tug *Triton* also of Falmouth. The barque arrived at Falmouth about mid-day.

Others of this hardy breed were not as fortunate as those in the previous incident. In January 1908 St Mawes pilots John Andrew and Richard Green of the cutter *Vincent* were drowned, dragged down by the heavy coats and sea-boots commonly worn in winter and adverse weather. Their small punt, launched from the cutter, was upset on heavy seas off the Lizard as, with deck-hand Richard Greet, they were approaching the German 474-ton schooner *Eduard* which had raised a signal flag for a pilot. John Andrew vanished quickly, and the two other pilots left on the cutter, James Williams and James Dash, made valiant but unsuccessful efforts to save Green. Meanwhile, Harry Morrison, single-handed in his brand-new Falmouth quay punt *Melville*, only launched from R.S. Burt's yard a few days previously, was out 'seeking' ships. The conditions were such that he was using a small jib and mizzen with two reefs in the mainsail. On seeing the incident he managed to approach and secure the weakening Richard Greet, eventually lifting him single-handed into the boat, apparently by using a rope as a parbuckle. (A loop of rope, one end fixed to the boat, is passed under the object which is then raised or rolled upwards by hauling on the free end. The effort in lifting is considerably reduced.) Fortunately during this time the design of the quay punt meant that she must have stayed quietly 'head to wind'. Eyewitness accounts of the tragedy appeared in the *Falmouth Packet* on 24 January, where Morrison was highly praised for his seamanship during the rescue of Richard Greet.

An unknown schooner of early deep-hulled type undergoing repairs on a gridiron at the entrance to Bar Creek prior to 1890. The workmen below are dwarfed by the massive hull which may have been built locally. (RCPS.)

SCHOONERS, KETCHES AND SMACKS

The types of small merchant vessels built in the shipyards of the Fal followed the national pattern. Square-rigged vessels predominated up until the late eighteenth century, from whence there was a gradual trend towards 'fore and aft' rig in the form of brigantines, schooners and ketches. Vessels such as this, incorporating improved design in hull shapes, could be faster, make better progress on windward passages and, needing fewer crew, were more economical to run. Schooner rig is said to have been first developed in Europe and later adopted and improved by North American and British builders. Although hull shapes varied depending on the requirements of the owner and techniques employed by the shipwright, from a distance most small schooners basically looked much the same. A schooner is defined as a vessel with one main mast and one fore mast, the latter usually slightly shorter than the main. (Schooners with two masts are not referred to as 'two-masted' but with more than two masts are referred to as three, four, or perhaps even five masted.) Main and foresails were gaff-rigged, with topsails; there was a sail on the fore stay and perhaps three jibs on the long bow-sprit. Most British schooners carried one or two square topsails on the fore mast for better down-wind performance and remained relatively small, for their trade took them to undeveloped shallow harbours and creeks at home or abroad. They could be kedged or towed into a mud berth for the transfer of cargo, whether it might be timber from a Norwegian fiord, dried cod from a Newfoundland River port, or copper ore from a quay in the local Restronguet Creek.

A dramatic picture of an unknown schooner, in which the versatility of the rig is admirably demonstrated. To ride out the gale the foresail, topgallant and outer jib have been stowed. To balance the rig the mainsail has been reefed and the tack triced up. Three crew appear to be at the long tiller. Let us hope that the cargo below didn't comprise sixty cattle from Spain. (NMM Cornwall.)

In the first quarter of the nineteenth century South Devon harbours were producing more schooners than anywhere else in the country; merchants in Penryn, Truro and Falmouth were soon demanding similar craft from local yards. By this time manuals had been published containing plans and sections of hulls and lay-out of rigging and sails, therefore shipwrights could quickly adopt the new designs. The size of vessel built depended on what it was to be used for, varying from *Stag* of 48 registered tons built by Symons on the Bar in 1824, to the exceptional *Mary Barrow* by Lean in 1891 of 164 tons. The busiest period of schooner building on the Fal was between 1840 and 1880. Lean's *Mary Barrow* and the steel *C & F Nurse* were rare exceptions after that period.

The first reference to a schooner built at a Fal shipyard appeared in the advertisement (overleaf) for the sale of the Bluett yard in 1802, although at less than 9m in length it could hardly be classed as a merchant vessel. However, the advantages of the new 'fore and aft' rig over the traditional square-sailed brig type was not lost on the local merchants. Schooners could point up much higher towards the wind than was possible for square sails, saving time and money otherwise spent making long tacks towards prevailing winds such as the westerlies in the English Channel.

In May 1827 an advertisement for a new shipping company, operating schooners, appeared in the *Royal Cornwall Gazette*. (A year later the company were also operating the smacks *Star, Four Friends* and *Harmony*. A rival company was the London, Falmouth, Penryn, Union Co., trading between Cotton's Wharf, London and Peter Roger's Wharf, Penryn, with schooners *Fanny, Enterprise* and *Active*.)

A three-masted schooner lies off the beach at Percuil, inland from St Mawes. At low water cargo such as coal would be discharged into carts by using the moveable chute hung on the port side. (RCPS.)

NEW SHIPPING COMPANY

'The Falmouth, Penryn, Helston, Redruth and
General Commercial Company
Respectfully announce
to the public that their first vessel called
THE PENDENNIS
is launched, and will sail for
HAYS' WHARF, LONDON
in about ten days – The second called
THE FALMOUTH
was launched on Saturday the 12th instant
and will sail in due course.
The Third to be called
THE CARN-BREA
Is in a state of forwardness, and will follow the
others, and henceforward a regular succession
of the Company's Vessels will trade to and
from Falmouth, Penryn and London, at stated
periods of short duration. The Committee
feel it is their duty to state …. that they have
succeeded in procuring from the Builders…
Such Vessels as are (if not superior to any)
inferior to none …. J. Ellis, Secretary, Falmouth.'

Schooner alongside Exchequer Quay, Penryn at low water. On the far side of the creek is Freeman's extensive granite works, where thousands of tons of stone from the nearby quarries was dressed and shipped out for building projects in Britain and abroad. (RCPS.)

The advertisement inferred that nearly one hundred people had become shareholders, however with the lack of information it is not known if they received any dividend. In September 1835 Ellis advertised the auction of all three vessels. The contracts for building *Pendennis* and *Carn-Brea* had been given to James Dunn of Mevagissey. Since the beginning of the century he had been in partnership with or employed first-class shipwrights to build or repair a great variety of vessels at Port Mellon, an inlet just to the west of Mevagissey. Dunn had much experience in operating fast vessels, particularly big cutters. This was the type of vessel used on smuggling runs from Cornwall to Guernsey and beyond, and also used by the revenue men, for in earlier days Dunn had been one of the foremost smugglers in the West Country. By 1827 he had become more respectable but with legal and financial problems; the order for two schooners was most welcome. *Pendennis* and *Carn-Brea* had identical dimensions: 55ft (16m) in length with 10ft (3m) draft, they were registered at 81 tons. The third vessel, *Falmouth*, was built by Francis Symons at the Bar, Falmouth. She had exactly the same dimensions as the others, therefore Symons was working to the same plans as supplied to Port Mellon. These early West Country schooners were quite short compared to their draft and beam. Improved designs, already in use elsewhere, were generally longer, faster and could carry more cargo but still with a draft of only 10ft (3m) or so. In 1834 Merchants G.C. Fox & Co. had to go to a yard at Bridport in Dorset to obtain the *Trefusis*, a larger schooner of 124 tons, for trading to the Baltic and Mediterranean. From 1845 until at least 1866 this vessel was owned and operated mainly on coastal work by the Hitchens family of Falmouth. Through the availability of design manuals, the introduction of better building materials, and spread

Three schooners and a barquentine (right) lie to anchors on the Flushing side of the harbour, *c.*1900.
The town quay is in the centre of the waterfront and the Bar to the left. (RCPS.)

of knowledge generated by the movement of qualified apprentices along the coast, the
shipyards of the Fal were soon able to produce a great variety of excellent schooners.

During the second half of the nineteenth century small steam-powered cargo boats,
with efficient and reliable engines, began to be used for coastal work. Railways and an
improving road system also posed a threat to the traditional coastal trade. To try to cut
their costs and compete with lower freight charges, some merchant sailing craft owners
purchased generally smaller ketches, or converted their schooners to this lighter and
more easily handled rig. They could therefore employ fewer crew and save some money
on wages. Many also had auxiliary engines fitted which made cargo delivery times more
predictable. Ketch rig basically consists of a main sail on the fore mast and a smaller one
on the mizzen mast towards the stern, both usually fitted with top sails, plus a stay-sail and
a couple of jibs on the bow-sprit. Although on the Fal several schooners were converted
to ketch rig, there are remarkably few records of local shipwrights building new ketches.
However, there was one remarkable exception, but in this case the vessels were not built
for trading, but for fishing.

In the early nineteenth century the sea fishermen of Brixham in South Devon were
already circumnavigating Britain in the search for new fishing grounds. To this end their
local shipwrights developed powerful sailing trawlers capable of coping with some of the
worst seas in the world. Their earlier small square-rigged craft evolved into luggers, which
in turn were succeeded by single-masted gaff-rigged cutters, generally known as smacks

or sloops. In about 1840 a rich fishing ground was found by accident to the south of the Dogger Bank off the East Coast. Huge catches of sole and other species were obtained in an area to be called the Silver Pits. To the fishermen of Devon it was their Klondike. Many, possibly up to a thousand in a decade, pulled up their roots and migrated to the East Coast, settling in Hull and Scarborough, the nearest ports to the fishing grounds. In 1854 there were thirty smacks in Hull; within ten years this number had grown to 270, and by 1880 there were 420. As trawls became larger and were fished deeper, more powerful vessels, up to 80ft (24m) in length, were required. With a second mast and sails added many therefore became ketch-rigged, and similar in appearance to today's few remaining Brixham smacks. The bonanza was not without its price: North Sea storms could wreak havoc among the fleet, smacks were sunk or severely damaged and many lives lost. But fishing carried on and vessels, at least, could be replaced. All around the coast shipyards were receiving orders for smacks.

The Fal was to receive a number of such orders, however they were not given to one of the established yards but to Emanuel Martin. No earlier local records of him have been traced, therefore he may have gained experience and a good reputation elsewhere and moved to the district. In 1877 Martin began building at Mylor, on the west side of the estuary. The exact location of his yard is unknown, possibly along the shallow Mylor Creek or at the small ex-Royal Naval repair and victualling yard, now Mylor Yacht Harbour. This dockyard had provided refitting facilities during the Napoleonic War and later for hull re-coppering of packet vessels. By the 1870s it was a shore base for the static training ship HMS *Ganges*, moored off St Just on the other side of the estuary. Obviously the infrastructure for shipbuilding was available at the dockyard if a small area could be rented in the short term. At least one ketch had already been built at Mylor: W. Withey built the 92-ton smack *Garland* somewhere here in 1855, using it himself for coastal work. Another was to be constructed during 1878 at Trelew, an inlet on the west side of Mylor Creek, Thomas Gray launching the 75-ton *Hobah* from there in March 1879. Gray used the ketch for European trade and for cargoes of Penryn granite for harbour works at Gibraltar. Later owners fitted her with an auxiliary engine and she carried on trading in coastal waters until the 1930s.

In 1878, as Gray was working on *Hobah* somewhere at Mylor, possibly the dockyard, Emanuel Martin was building two 79-ton ketch-rigged fishing smacks for Hull owners, the *Lily of the West* and the *Lock Fyne*. In the same year a third order for a similar vessel, the *Valiant*, was given to Henry Trethowan, by that time working at the Bar, Falmouth. The quality of Martin's work generated further orders, and he was obliged to seek larger premises, successfully tendering for the tenancy of an old shipbuilding yard and dry dock at Ponsharden on the Penryn River. During the next decade Emanuel Martin & Co. built a further seven smacks of between 79 and 90 tons for Hull owners; *Evangeline, Integrity, Eagle Wing, Intrepid, Garnett Brothers, Daisy* and *Good Hope*. In 1880, for a change, he also built the 77-ton auxiliary-engined *Penryn* for local owners. *Penryn* was trading in coastal waters until the Second World War, when she became a floating platform for a barrage balloon defending Falmouth Harbour. In 1886 Martin built his largest vessel, the wooden-hulled 102-ton steam trawler *Laurel* for Hull owners. In spite of such a prolific output, in 1891 Martin was reported to have gone bankrupt.

Above: A large ketch at beautiful Percuil. Two horses harnessed in tandem cool their hooves while the cart is loaded. All sails are neatly furled and secured with gaskets and clear of the deck for cargo handling. This is facilitated with a gin block hung between the masts. (RCPS)

Left: This damaged but important photograph is of Captain Edwin Hutchings, in 1900 Master of the 88 -ton ketch *Francis* which was built by Charles Burt & Sons on the Bar in 1889. The massiveness of the sailing gear is well illustrated by the wheel, the stowed mizzen boom, and the sheet tackle blocks behind the boom crutch. (Royal Institution of Cornwall.)

Some inkling of the terrible loss of lives and vessels among the East Coast fishing fleets may be gathered from the records of the few Falmouth-built vessels. The number lost through collision, probably with other trawlers, illustrates that many were gathering in close proximity on the grounds, by night as well as day. In 1888 *Valiant* was lost in a collision 200 miles east of Spurn Head (the mouth of the Humber); in 1893 *Garnett Brothers* was lost in a collision with a steam trawler 240 miles east north east of Spurn; in 1894 *Lily of the West* sank from collision in the North Sea; and in 1899 *Daisy* was lost off Southwold.

Apart from the many 'deep water' merchant vessels built on the Fal there were also small sailing barges for use within the harbour and creeks of the estuary. These were sloop- or cutter-rigged, often with running bowsprits. Sizes varied between 10m long, 16-ton vessels, up to about 15m, of 25 tons registry. Cargo capacity could be up to about double the registered tonnage. They were near-flat-bottomed beamy craft, capable of taking the ground on beach or creek-side for transfer of cargo, but being Fal-built were also good sailing vessels. They were often owned by millers, coal or timber merchants, but shares, as with other trading vessels, could be distributed among families or local businessmen. Crew consisted of two men, perhaps father and son, assisted at times by labourers for loading and unloading. This was facilitated by the use of a separate gaff spar which acted as a derrick crane. This was raised up the mast using the throat and peak halyards which had been un-shackled from the gaff yard of the mainsail which was left stowed on the boom. Cargo was raised from the hold by means of a wire or strong line through a gin block hung from the gaff down to a dolly-winch or tackle at the mast foot or on the bow. Guy ropes swung the gaff to the required position over hold or quay. Intimate knowledge of the shallow winding channels was required for barges to reach tiny quays at the highest point of tidal creeks, usually without an engine. Often they had to be shoved up with the tide, using poles perhaps of over 7m in length. Much of the trade consisted of agricultural products, sand, stone, bricks, timber, coal and grain; some of which was transhipped from vessels in Falmouth Docks.

There are practically no records of the building of these craft, although most of the local yards probably built one or two. With a little assistance a bargeman might construct a vessel on a beach for his own use, leaving no record, apart perhaps from its name on the transom, seen on an old family photograph. Vessels of that size were seldom included in the *Mercantile Navy List* or on the *Lloyd's Register*. Some representative barges include *Arwenack*, of 34 tons, built in 1796, probably on the Bar, at one time used for harbour dredging, and *William and Alfred*, of 22 tons, built by Symons on the Bar in 1815 for merchants Broad & Co. One of the few sizeable vessels built in St Mawes was the 16-ton *Commerce*, launched by William Peters in 1832. At Devoran, H.E. Stephens built the 15-ton *Annie* in 1870, and five years later the *Mary*, of 25 tons. The principal initial shareholder of *Mary* was Thomas Hicks of Truro with thirty-two shares. A merchant, accountant and agent, all of Devoran, and a ship owner of Falmouth, had eight shares each. She was known as a 'little big barge', a cross between the small 'inside' barges and the 'outside' barges which were sea-worthy enough for coastal voyages around the Lizard and to Fowey and Plymouth. *Mary* had a long and varied career, which fortunately was documented by Basil Greenhill and David MacGregor in *The Mariners Mirror*.[1]

Above: Barge *Swift* of Truro, with boarding punt in tow, heavily laden with sacks of grain or similar cargo trans-shipped in Falmouth Docks. She drifts past the Northern Breakwater towards the open water of Carrick Roads and the mills of Truro beyond. (Royal Institution of Cornwall.)

Left: Ketch-rigged barge *Eclipse*. Her sails may be worn and well-patched but they have been well set and drawing nicely. The big topsail on a deceptively delicate mast was essential for catching the fickle winds when navigating narrow tree-bordered creeks. (RCPS.)

The larger Fal craft were similar to the ketch and smack-rigged barges of the Tamar, two of the surviving craft from that river being *Shamrock* and *Garlandstone*. Fal outside barges include the 18-ton, 13m-long sloop *Fanny*, launched by John Stephens at Carnon Yard, Restronguet in 1877. She was used by R.S. Hitchens of Truro and later sold to Plymouth owners for coastal work, probably for carrying stone, for she was wrecked near the Lizard in 1907. Another was the 32-ton smack *Mystery*, built by Charles Dyer at Sunny Corner, Truro in 1885. Others were *Cornish Lass*, of 35 tons, built for the Tamar by J.T. Rapson at Penryn in 1900. Rapson also built the 27-ton cutter *Inez* in 1894, and the shapely 25-ton ketch *Lily* in 1897.

After a few years owned by Philip Dawe in Penryn, *Lily* spent the rest of her time under Ilfracombe and Bideford owners, trading to small ports around the Bristol Channel and River Severn. Edmund Eglinton in *Last of the Sailing Coasters* vividly describes his time as mate aboard 'the lively little *Lily*' in the 1920s, when times were hard and owners were cutting costs to the bone. An auxiliary engine had once been installed but since had been neglected and, like the motor winch, had rusted up. Therefore the skipper and mate, working for near-subsistence wages, had to, and preferred to, use traditional and very specialised sailing skills needed in those treacherous shallow tidal waters. *Lily* was ideal for negotiating narrow muddy creeks to isolated country wharfs, drawing about 1½m when light, but could carry 60 tons of Welsh coal, at that time her principal cargo. This was shovelled out of her hold, perhaps onto a beach, sometimes by skipper and mate alone. This hard but immensely satisfying way of life succumbed to road transportation: *Lily* was laid up on the River Yeo; last recorded in the *Mercantile Navy List* in 1926.

The 32-ton ketch *Eclipse* was built on the Penryn River in 1892, builder not known, but probably Rapson. Initially bought by a Plymouth shipping company, in the 1930s she was owned and skippered by Norman Morrison, his son Jimmy crewing. The Morrison family played an important part in the life of maritime Falmouth, on barging, fishing, oyster-dredging, pleasure-tripping and working with quay punts. Jimmy's uncle, Walter 'Peaceful' Morrison, owned *I.C.U.*, perhaps the most famous and successful quay punt.

Much of the trade of the *Eclipse* consisted of 'stone-hacking', carrying roadstone which was crushed 'blue elvan' rock, a type of igneous gabbro from the coastal quarries at Porthoustock on the Lizard. From time to time a number of sailing barges were involved in this trade during the 1930s; several from Plymouth included the famous *Shamrock*. Laden barges, carrying perhaps 60 tons or so, would work up to Port Navas and Gweek on the Helford River, or to quays at Penryn, St Mawes, Truro and Tresillian. The most important thing was to get the tide right and 'trying to keep off the mud'. With the help of a winch and tackle from the gaff spar and two hired labourers, 60 tons, in 2.5 hundredweight wicker baskets, could be discharged in three hours. If they had the tide right they could catch the rest of the ebb to get back to Porthoustock to load the following day. At the unloading quays there were mixers for stone and tar which was distributed throughout West Cornwall as macadam, creating paved roads which had previously been no more than gravel tracks. Thereby the bargemen assisted the introduction of motorised road transport which hastened the demise of working sail.

RESTRONGUET AND PILL CREEKS

A lone contemporary shipping note has survived regarding a coal delivery to Truro at the height of the Industrial Revolution; the coal had been ordered by John Mitchell & Co. who were merchants in Truro with major interests in mining and smelting. The partnership of Robert and William Mitchell ran the large lead smelting works at Point on Restronguet Creek from 1830, and another brother, John, the tin smelting works at Calenick Creek, just to the south of Truro, the probable destination of the coal. The printed note, with names, date and destination added by pen, reads:

> Shipped in good order and condition by the Newport Coal Company, in and upon the good vessel called the *Merton* of Truro whereof Samuel Hayes is Master for this present voyage, now riding at anchor in the Port of Newport, and bound for Truro, to say one hundred and seventeen tons of coal … are to be delivered in like good order and condition, at the aforesaid Port of Truro (all and every the Dangers and Accidents of the Seas and Navigation, of whatever Nature or Kind soever excepted) unto Messrs. John Mitchell and Co. or their assigns, he or they paying freight for the said goods… Dated in Newport, the Twentieth day of November 1841.

The *Merton* was a schooner of 93 tons, built in Swansea in 1826 and acquired by Mitchell before 1833 for trade between Truro and South Wales. Over the preceding centuries strong links had been forged between the copper mining interests in Cornwall and the ore smelters and coal shippers of South Wales, where shipyards profited by building many vessels for the coastal and overseas coal trade. For instance, Welsh copper smelters such as Pascoe Grenfell & Sons, associates of Thomas Williams, the 'Copper King' and owner of the Parys copper mines on Anglesey, had Cornish agents and their own 'hutches' or ore shipment containers at the port of Devoran. In the other direction, G.C. Fox & Co., founders and owners until 1856 of the great Perran Foundry and merchants and shipping agents in Falmouth, also owned coal mines, iron-ore mines and foundries in Neath, South Wales, building tramways and quays for the shipment of cargoes there and at Portreath on the north coast of Cornwall. Their profits, made by men, women and children often working in horrific conditions in mines and smelting works, funded the establishment of some of the renowned exotically planted gardens of Cornwall.

Some idea of trade on the upper reaches of the Fal in the Victorian era may be gained from the weekly shipping reports in local newspapers. In August 1853, in one typical week at the height of the tin and copper mining in West Cornwall, eight coal ships from South Wales arrived in the Port of Truro, much of the cargo probably destined for the steam engines which kept the mines operating. Other ships brought goods from Gloucester, Plymouth and London. During the same week, on Restronguet Creek ships lay in the deep-water pool near the 'Passage House' (now a well-known tourist venue called the Pandora Inn), before taking their turn to move up on high tide to Point Quay, the terminus of the mineral railway serving the mines of Gwennap. No less than nineteen vessels, from Cardiff, Swansea, Newport, Llanelly, Port Talbot and Neath, delivered cargoes to Point, most probably exchanging cargoes of coal and iron for copper ore.

A telephoto view looking inland across Restronguet Pool at low water, 2006. The shallowness of the creek above here is obvious. Strangweke Quay is on the left, Yard Point to the right, and the quays of Point central in the background.

Nearly two decades later, a report in the *West Briton* newspaper in March 1873 emphasised that the Fal quays were still essential for the mining industry and import of general merchandise. In an exceptional ten days in March there arrived at Malpas, the height of navigation for the larger vessels such as barques and barquentines with cargoes for Truro, twenty coasters chiefly with coal, an English three-masted schooner from Iquique, Chile, with nitrate of soda, six French vessels with grain and flour, and sixteen Norwegian with timber. Much of the latter was destined for the mines, via Harvey's timber ponds and saw mills in Truro. At the same time some ship-loads were discharged at Restronguet Pool, destined to be rafted up to roadside quays near the Perran Foundry on the little Kennal River at the head of Restronguet Creek. At other times goods could be off-loaded at Strangeweke Quay (near the Pandora Inn) and taken further inland through shallower water to the Perran or Devoran wharves by small barges. This quay had been part of the infrastructure of the Perran Foundry since its establishment by the Fox family, and vital for the export by sea of manufactured products such as boilers and mine machinery. The foundry's last Cornish pumping engine was exported from here in 1880. In July that year a notice appeared in the *West Briton* advertising the sale of the foundry including the quay, which was said to have access for vessels of 200 tons (at high water), with a powerful crane thereon, capable of lifting 25 tons. The quay and small dock still serve a useful purpose, providing a summer base for yacht tenders and sailing dinghies.

Restronguet Creek is now populated by migrant wildfowl in winter and pleasure craft in summer, most of the latter going nowhere except up and down with the tide. Its peaceful charm gives little hint of the abuse it received during centuries of mining activities. For many generations man dug for alluvial tin along the little Carnon River which discharges into the head of the creek, even excavating shafts below the bed of the creek itself for the rich deposits washed down the valley throughout the ages. Thousands of tons of mine

Devoran, 2006, looking towards Point and Carrick Roads. A dredged channel, wharves and railway lines would have once occupied the site. The copper ore 'hutches' on the left are reminders of this once highly industrialised site.

waste were deposited in the creek, seen today at low water as cumulative banks of sand, gravel and mud dissected by meandering streams from the valleys. Nevertheless, in the first half of the nineteenth century an inland industrial port was created at the hamlet of Devoran on the north side of the creek. It served as the terminus of the Redruth and Chasewater Railway (before the tramway extension to Point), having extensive quays, a coalyard, limekiln, brickworks, stables, engine sheds and quayside storage bins or 'hutches' where copper ore shipments were stored. Small merchantmen either under sail or steam powered reached here at high tide to discharge coal, roadstone, timber and mining materials, leaving with ore for the smelters in South Wales. In the 1870s there was even a shipyard at the lower end of the quays where H.E. Stephens, father and son, distantly related to John Stephens of Yard Point, built the Fal barge *Mary* and at least two large schooners, *Mary and Julia* and *Maggie*. In spite of dredging there were always problems with silting of the navigation channel and with the collapse of the Cornish mining industry the port was quickly abandoned. In the twentieth century the many creekside industrial works were swept away and adapted or replaced by desirable rural housing. A few industrial ruins, such as the stone-built ore storage hutches and fragments of mine engine houses survive, now protected by the local conservation society.

Apart from its reputation as an inland port, Restronguet also became known for shipbuilding. Early in the nineteenth century shipwright Peter Ferris built small barges and at least one schooner on a spit of land on the south side of the entrance to the muddy Penpol Creek: this was known as Yard Point, also confusingly known as Carnon Yard,

Right: Barge *Mary* sits in a mud berth at Devoran. The robust rigging and high topmast seem to confirm her reputation for fast coastal sailing. The mainsail spars have been swung well to starboard to facilitate unloading of cargo which may be roadstone from the Lizard quarries, possibly in the early twentieth century. (RCPS.)

Below: A roadside wharf on the Perran River at the head of Restronguet Creek. The small 'inside' barge is rigged very lightly compared to *Mary*. It carries a barrel windlass forward of the mast. The cargo-handling gaff and gin block is set for unloading . (RCPS.)

where a mine engine house once stood. Here, and probably at Pill Creek, a narrow inlet at the head of Carrick Roads, Peter's son, Thomas, built a number of merchant vessels. The site today, a rocky foreshore with scrubland behind it, bears little trace of what was achieved there, apart from a plaque erected by the local conservation society. In the 1850s Thomas launched a number of schooners, including *Clipper* (88 tons), *William Henry* (87 tons, possibly enlarged to 102 tons), *Cock'o the Walk* (143 tons) and *JST* (127 tons). Viv Acton in *Life by the Fal* quotes an eyewitness account of the tragic loss of this last vessel in a gale off Hartland Point, North Devon, in November 1864. The captain and six crew lost their lives. The records are littered with references to similar ends to beautiful vessels and their crews. A more long-lived vessel was *Mary Ann* a 31-ton lugger built for the St Ives fishing fleet in 1856, a type not normally associated with the Fal shipwrights. She lasted until New Year's Day 1912, when she also was lost.

Thomas Ferris became bankrupt in 1858 and the yard was purchased by John Stephens. His first vessel was the small schooner *Primus*, of 59 tons. William Ferris, Thomas's son, was employed as yard foreman, having served his apprenticeship at Yard Point and Pill Creek. Within a few years he became renowned as an excellent designer and shipwright. A selection of some of his vessels includes the 62-ton schooner *Racer*, built in 1866 and registered in Fowey for St Austell owners. Her trade obviously took her to the Mediterranean for she was wrecked on Crete in 1889. The well-known *Rhoda Mary* of 130 tons was launched in 1868 for Captain John Mayrick's company in Falmouth and under various owners she traded to the Baltic and Mediterranean. In 1898 she was re-rigged with a third mast: smaller sails and yards gave greater versatility and easier work for the crew. A model of *Rhoda Mary* is featured in an historical display in the new maritime museum in Falmouth, and another at the Cotehele Quay museum on the River Tamar. Other schooners include the three masted *Lizzie R. Wilce*, the largest William Ferris vessel at 155 tons, launched in 1876 for Elijah Wilce of Falmouth. Voyages took her to South Africa and the West Indies for fruit. By 1883 she was owned by the local Chellew family of timber merchants. This vessel came to an unfortunate end on Porthminster Beach, St Ives during a gale in January 1908. The 107-ton *Hetty* was built for Chellew in 1877: as timber merchants the company may have used her for the Baltic trade but she is also recorded as sailing to the Mediterranean. She was one of the few long-lived schooners, having an auxiliary 21hp paraffin engine fitted in 1926, by which time there were very few small commercial vessels under sail. She kept working until 1935 when finally she had to be abandoned when sinking in the Bristol Channel. John Stephens gave up the yard in 1880, but 'Foreman' Ferris carried on until the twentieth century building smaller fishing and pleasure craft here and possibly at Pill Creek.

The Pill shipyard was on the east side of the creek where there exists a long beautifully built stone wharf and slipways fronting a levelled platform of land. Here the creek once saw trains of mules bringing panniers of copper ore to the wharf for transportation by schooners and brigantines to South Wales. William Ferris' grandfather, the first Peter Ferris, built several Fal barges and other vessels at Pill in the early part of the nineteenth century. His grandson, Peter, the elder brother of William, built the 54-ton smack *Charles Gray* here in 1861 and the 129-ton schooner *Deerfoot* in 1862; he then became a shipwright in Charlestown. Meanwhile W. Hodge had taken over at Pill, launching the

Low tide at Pill Creek, 2006, depicting the wharf, shipbuilding yard and slipways. The nearest cottage was once an inn, dispensing ale to thirsty mariners, pack-horse teamsters and shipbuilders.

128-ton schooner *Glenfeadon* in 1863 and the even larger 177-ton *A.D. Gilbert* two years later. He was followed by the firm of Hitchens & Ford. Frank Hitchens built the 94-ton schooner *Reaper* in 1875, the 100-ton *JWT* in 1877, and the 97-ton *Lizzie Edith* two years later. Such vessels were soon to become a thing of the past as shippers turned to the greater reliability and speed of steam power, and shipwrights working in wood had to increasingly turn to orders for smaller working craft and yachts.

A good number of oyster-dredging boats were once based on these sheltered waters. Therefore it is understandable that the local shipwrights built here some of the best Truro River oyster boats or 'Falmouth working boats' as they are now commonly called. Oyster dredging has been carried out on the Fal for hundreds of years. There are not the number of fishermen today as in former times, but in recent years in the winter season perhaps a score of boats might be working. There are two methods of dredging: in the narrower creeks and reaches of the Fal oar-driven 'haultow' punts (5m-long rowing boats) are used. The fisherman drops overboard an anchor on a running line, rows away on his chosen course for perhaps 100m, drops a dredge overboard, then using a hand windlass winds his way back to the anchor dredging across the oyster bed as he goes. The other method is by towing perhaps several dredges behind specialised sailing boats across the wide open waters of Carrick Roads. Both disciplines require an intimate knowledge of the bed of the estuary and its tides and highly skilled boat handling. Falmouth has probably the last fishing fleet in Europe which operates under sail alone. Although nowadays some of the craft have engines to take them to and from the dredging areas, it was agreed several generations ago to only use sail to conserve the oyster stocks. A variety of small fishing

One of a number of haul and tow punts dredging the oyster beds in 2006. The dredge lies on the stern thwart and the frame of the 'wink' or winch is supported on the forward thwart. The fisherman stands facing the bow to wind the central winch handle.

craft were once used for this work, but since Victorian times the unique locally built long-keeled gaff cutters have dominated the fishery.

William Ferris made a number of oyster boats, either at Yard Point or Pill, including a rare survival *Florence*, built in 1895. She is now owned by a St Mawes syndicate of enthusiasts and after an extensive rebuild is racing again. Frank Hitchens' work survives today in the form of several oyster boats with an average length of 8m: *Shadow*, initially built in 1870 and still working from Mylor; *Royal Oak*, renamed *Victory*, which is still winning her class, and *Evelyn*, raced by a Roseland syndicate. The smaller *Softwing*, which Frank Hitchens built in 1900, was purchased and restored to her original appearance by the Cornish Maritime Trust, who still exhibit and sail her in the summer months. The Trust also own and maintain two other important boats, *Ellen*, a Gorran Haven crabber built in 1882, and *Barnabus*, a 40ft (12m) St Ives mackerel driver, one of the very few traditional Cornish fishing luggers remaining. At the time of writing, with the assistance

Part of the oyster fleet dredging in a brisk northerly breeze off Loe Beach in December 2005. *Shadow, Boy Willie* and *Six Brothers* drift across with dropped staysails, roller-reefed and scandalised mainsails and storm jibs.

Dolly, named *Five Sisters* when built in 1914, dredging with reefed mainsail and drooping jib on tightened-down bowsprit. December 2005.

of a generous grant, she is undergoing a major rebuild at Penzance. Thereafter she will have to be supported by the dedication of Trust members, who will be recompensed by sailing this magnificent, powerful vessel.

THE UPPER FAL

Sea voyagers sailing into the broad expanse of the Fal Estuary for the first time may be forgiven for thinking that apart from their seaward entrance they are entering a vast enclosed bay encompassed by a continuous shoreline. Once past St Mawes to starboard and Falmouth town and the Penryn River to port, there seems to be no break in the surrounding hills, which rise steeply from the shore on either side. To the west and north the parishes of Mylor and Feock consist of agricultural land interspersed with planted woodland and scattered houses of the fortunate. The rich farming countryside of the Roseland lies to the east. From sea level the slopes rise to heights of about 80m, and although interlaced with deep hidden valleys, from a distance Roseland appears as a remarkably level landscape. The surrounding view is entirely man-made, except at the northern end of the bay where stunted oaks clinging to the rocky shore hint at a wilder scene somewhere beyond. The skipper of a large vessel navigating these waters must stick to the buoyed deep-water channel, avoiding the shallows off St Mawes, Mylor, Messack and Restronguet. Otherwise, within reason and allowing for the rise and fall of 5m at spring tides, a yachtsman with a 1m draft boat has at least 10sq.km of estuary to play on.

   Several kilometres within the roadstead, the observant voyager may begin to discern tantalising breaks in the shore-line. Mylor Creek lies to the west behind the tree-clad hill of Greatwood, its narrow entrance close by the beautiful little medieval church hidden, particularly in the summer, by the massed ranks of yacht masts at Mylor Harbour. On the opposite side of the estuary, St Just Pool, backed by its extensive shingle bar, scarcely breaks the sky-line. It is 2km away by water, and about fifteen by road, via the King Harry Ferry. From a boat one has to scramble ashore across a sea-weedy and sandy beach before the medieval church and its beautiful sub-tropical gardens come into view. Passing Greatwood, it is not until your boat may be on a course towards Carick Carlys Rock (marked with cardinal posts) which guards its entrance, that Restronguet Creek may be glimpsed beyond the Pandora Inn and more tethered yachts. Houses of various styles, each isolated amid a great variety of trees, occupy the slopes at the northern end of the roadstead. They lie within the parish of Feock, although little can be seen of the village and church tucked away behind the trees. At tide level more yachts cluster before shingly Loe Beach, accessible from the village by a precipitous narrow lane, but a magnet for picnickers and dinghy sailors in the holiday season. Further eastwards now: barely visible in the now rock-bound shore, the entrance to tiny Pill Creek beckons the more adventurous small-boat sailor. Winds can be fickle at this end of Carrick Roads, but generally there is safe sailing. However, with strong winds from the east and more especially the south, coupled with an ebbing tide, big swells can build up, with uncomfortable choppy seas developing at the shallower and narrowing northern end.

1 The harbour entrance: St Anthony headland from Little Dennis Fort, Pendennis.

2 St Anthony Lighthouse and headland.

3 The Falmouth pilot boat *L.K. Mitchell*, delivering pilots to visiting ships since 1978. She was replaced in December 2006 by the powerful motor-launch *Arrow*, named after the earlier sailing cutter.

4 Pendennis Castle.

5 Carrick Roads from Pendennis.

6 A ship passes St Mawes en route to the dry docks. A less common sight is the nearer sailing vessel, a visiting Falmouth quay punt.

7 St Mawes.

8 The Queen Elizabeth Dock.

9 The National Maritime Museum, Cornwall.

10 The *Rhoda Mary,* the well-known schooner built on the Fal. Model in Cotehele Quay Maritime Museum, River Tamar. There is an unrigged version in the NMMC.

11 Falmouth from the tower of the National Maritime Museum, Cornwall.

12 Visiting Brixham trawlers *Leader* and *Provident*, now charter vessels but reminders of similar trading craft which once used the Town Quay beyond.

13 The High Street waterfront, site of war-time ship building by the Falmouth Boat Construction Company.

14 Flushing.

15 This smart quay punt was built by Thomas Jackett at his Falmouth High Street yard in 1912. Originally named *Nada*, now, confusingly, she is another *Curlew*.

16 The Cornish Maritime Trust working boat *Softwing*, with small jib and scandalised mainsail, demonstrating oyster dredging.

17 For several years racing Falmouth working boats had to negotiate this oil rig parked off Trefusis Point. (Flushing Regatta, 1994).

18 *Grace* and *Demelza* at close quarters, July 2006. Stylish G.R.P. working boats are still produced at Heard's Tregatreath boatyard on Mylor Creek.

19 *Boy Willie* and *Dolly* at rest at Mylor after winter dredging.

20 Repairs to working boat *Magdalena*, built at Mevagissey in about 1890.

21 Mylor medieval church.

22 The memorial to the *Queen* tragedy, situated in Mylor churchyard.

23 A buoy in Carrick Roads for ship mooring and cormorant roosting.

24 The bar and creek, St Just.

25 Low water on Mylor Creek

26 Tugs assisting the 6,500-ton refrigerated cargo vessel *Magnolia* round Turnaware Bar, August 1995.

27 Roundwood Quay and Cowlands Creek.

28 The Plymouth-built charter ketch *Bessie Ellen* at Tolverne, returning to waters where she once traded.

29 The Upper Fal, approaching Ruan Lanihorne at high tide.

30 Malpas.

31 Tresillian mud.

32 The way to Truro.

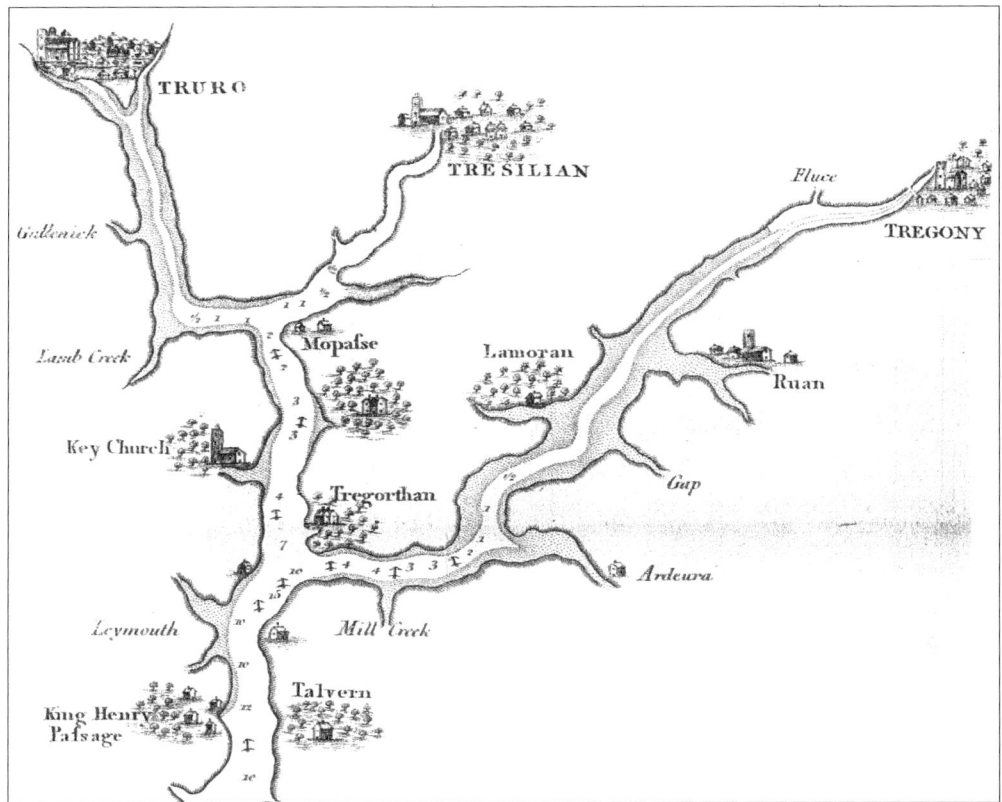

Map of the Upper Fal. Greenvile Collins' chart of 1697 adapted by Gilbert, 1817. It gives a very basic layout of the creeks. 'Mopafse' is Malpas Ferry, the modern settlement is on the north bank. 'Tregorthan' is Lord Falmouth's estate of Tregothnan. Roundwood and Cowland's Creek are at Leymouth (Lamouth Creek). Tolvern Pool is at that junction. (Cornwall Centre.)

The next feature to catch the eye is a large portico-fronted house on the summit of rising meadowland beyond a small bay. The situation was obviously chosen to have unparalleled views of the estuary to Pendennis and the sea 8km to the south. This is the mansion of Trelissick, the extensive estate of which is now managed by the National Trust. The estate had been purchased in about 1800 by R.A. Daniell of Truro who, following on from his father's association with mining baron William Lemon, increased the family fortune by investing in a highly productive copper mine near St Agnes on the north coast of Cornwall and a copper-smelting works at Llanelly in South Wales. He became Mayor of Truro and Member of Parliament for West Looe. His son Thomas proved to be very good at spending money: vast sums went on improvements to the estate and house. In 1823 it was largely rebuilt and embellished with a façade of six ionic columns topped by a triangular pediment, alleged to have been inspired by the temple of Erectheus in Athens, but in this situation more suitably dedicated to the god of copper. Later owners sold off some of the estate, but in 1955 nearly 400 acres surrounding the house were handed over to the National Trust. Now thousands of visitors annually enjoy the beautiful gardens, woods and parkland on the slopes above the Fal.

Channal's Creek and Trelissick House, 2006: a beautiful and sheltered anchorage for pleasure craft.

It appears we are now entering an enclosed bay, in the distance backed by a high cliff clothed in stunted oaks. A small green navigation buoy suddenly claims urgent attention. We are at Turnaware: on the starboard side a great bar of sand and shingle, with depths of less than ½m at low water on spring tides, extends half-way across the channel. We see that it *could* be a channel, for to the port of the buoy the depth-sounder reads 12m! On his chart of 1597 Boazio calls this Turner Weer Point. Rather than referring to the channel turning, the name could be derived from a fisherman of that name who had a 'wear' or weir here. Early fish trap weirs have been recorded here, at Weir Point, Restronguet, and at Tolverne. They would have consisted of basket or net traps incorporated into timber staging similar to the Severn Estuary fish weirs, and primarily used for catching migrating salmon and sea trout. Long ago the Fal Rivers must have teemed with these fish, until they were driven out by mining pollution. Fortunately, vigorous legislation has brought improvements to water quality, and there are now small but increasing populations of migratory and coarse species in most of the main tributaries. In the winter months Turnaware is one of the haunts of the haultow punts. Oyster beds in the shallower areas where the sailing dredging boats cannot operate have for generations been worked by these small rowing boats. No further physical-fitness exercise is required after hauling a dredge across the beds for a few hours.

The tide is flooding, drawing us towards the cliffs and high ground closes around us. From a 2km-wide estuary we are suddenly in a rock-bound channel a mere 200m wide. Winds here can gust from various directions, and there is rarely enough steady breeze to take a sailing boat on the required course. But pick an advantageous tide and, if not in a hurry, one can row, paddle or have a free ride towards the hills. We drift round a bend and one of the geological wonders of Cornwall opens up before us: we have entered what is generally known as King Harry Reach. The gorge runs due north and south; an almost straight 15m-deep channel within steep rocks rising above on either side. The

King Harry Reach from the north, June 2006. The new car ferry, seen midway across the channel, had been in service for only a few days after being completed by Pendennis Shipyard at Falmouth Docks. The mussel farm pontoons lie beyond.

deep flooded valley, 1km in length, appears artificially made, as though blasted out by explosives, reminiscent of a cutting on the Panama Canal. However, natural forces have carved this channel through the Devonian rocks of Roseland, possibly assisted by a fault in the underlying strata.

It may have taken a million years for water to do its work. In the region to the north, during the Ice Age a watershed was formed, its rivers draining and eroding the land surface. In the area of Goss Moor, through which traffic on the main spine road of Cornwall now thunders, rich deposits of tin were left as the softer rocks were worn away. Eastwards, in the present St Austell district, granite rocks were worn down or rotted away by permafrost, water and chemical changes to form vast deposits of china clay or kaolin. The rivers flowed southwards: what we know today as the Fal rises in Goss Moor and meanders through the western edge of the clay country and on to Grampound and Tregony. The Tresillian River, a little to the west, from Indian Queens flows through Ladock and Tresillian. Further west, the Rivers Allen and Kenwyn tumble through steep valleys to Truro where they converge into the Truro River. All these tributaries combined at the northern side of the rocks of Roseland during the Ice Age, possibly forming a vast lake over Tolverne before eventually breaking through to form the gorge which still voids the headwaters into the Fal Estuary.

The jagged rock sides of the channel have long been softened by seaweeds, algae and trees; a variety of native and introduced specimens on the Trelissick Estate side and stunted native oaks clinging to the rocks on the starboard side. Halfway along the channel, past an unsightly mussel farm and new landing stage for water-borne visitors to Trelissick, the King Harry car ferry crosses the channel. The conspicuous chain ferry is the most recent in a long line of craft dating back to medieval times. Before the twentieth-century improvements to roads and introduction of motorised transport the crossing formed an essential link between the Roseland and the west of the county, although the steep inclines to the high ground on both sides must have tested animals hauling to market anything more than the lightest of loads. The name of the ferry originates from a now-ruined chapel in the narrow valley on the east side, built by holders of the Manor of Tolverne and dedicated to the murdered King Henry VI. Earlier rowed ferry punts, which would have been difficult to operate when the tide was running fast, were replaced in 1888 by the first chain ferry powered by steam.

At the northern end of the reach lies the site of another ancient crossing from Tolverne on the Roseland across the Fal to Halwyn, Coombe and on through narrow lanes towards Truro. The steep sunken lane on the Halwyn side corroborates the tradition that Roseland cattle were swum across the river here on the way to Truro market. This ferry operated until the 1930s and since then the house has become known as 'Smugglers Cottage', popular tea-rooms and picnic destination for the Fal passenger excursion boats. At Tolverne the channel snakes eastwards and widens, being augmented by the union here of the Fal and Truro Rivers and to a lesser extent on the port side by the tiny Lamouth and Cowlands creeks. All is peace and tranquillity at the present time, especially in the winter months, but over the centuries Tolverne and its environs has seen much human activity in this seemingly remote area.

The wooded isthmus between the two creeks to port is called Roundwood, named as such because of the circular banks of the Iron Age settlement on the bluff above the creeks. The earthworks are similar to a large number of 'rounds' scattered throughout Cornwall. This one has an additional southern bank across the promontory but couldn't repel a serious attack. The site was more likely to have been a trading settlement rather than a heavily defended fort, perfectly sited in sheltered waters but with access to the sea for maritime commerce between the 'celtic' tribes of Gaul and the interior of Cornwall. In the latter part of the eighteenth century the position of Roundwood proved, in the short term, of some importance to the copper industry. On the narrow foreshore of this unlikely spot one of the few Cornish copper-smelting works was set up by the Chacewater Copper Company. Teams of pack-animals brought pannier-loads of ore across a hilly route of at least 10km from the mines of Gwennap. Large stone buildings and chimneys were erected on levelled ground below the fort, including five furnaces, two calciners and a lime kiln. For the ore refining process leats around the contours of the promontory led to a reservoir and waterwheel driving ore-crushing stamps. However, with the present apparent lack of a nearby natural water source it is difficult to know how a regular supply of water was obtained. The works existed for only a few years: the price of copper fell, and there were difficulties with the supply and maintenance of horse and mule teams over such a distance. An advertisement in the *Sherborne Mercury* in November 1798 offered the property for sale, including the wharf:

> The quays are new, and built in a most substantial manner, with excellent moor and moor-stone (granite) ribs and quoins; are upwards of 170ft in length and have, at the lowest tides, a depth of water sufficient for vessels of 300 tons to come alongside and unload, and any number of vessels may ride at anchor within the opposite basin in perfect safety. The wharfs are sufficiently large for the landing and disposing of any quantity of timber, coals, or other heavy articles and merchandise. There is a water course on each side of the main buildings,

King Harry Ferry, *c.*1910. The steam-powered pontoon discharges a Truro tradesman's van on the Roseland side. Laid-up ships, sheltered by the woods of Trelissick, almost block the passage up to Tolverne. (RCPS.)

Many ships were laid-up on the Fal during the 1930s Depression. (RCPS.)

supplied by a reservoir at a short distance, which will furnish water for any requisite purpose.

Subsequently R.A. Daniell of Trelissick acquired Roundwood, possibly reinstating for a time the pack-horse route, bringing copper ore to the wharf for export to South Wales and importing coal and timber. At about the same time he also established a wharf at Point on Restronguet Creek for the same purpose. Daniell was one of a number of Cornish mining barons who owned or controlled most of the huge smelting works in South Wales.

Apart from the possible use of the lime kiln the site languished as part of the pleasure grounds of Trelissick until the 1870s. The wharf was then taken over by the shipbuilder Henry Trethowan as an extension of his Little Falmouth yard. He may have built or repaired a number of vessels here, but only two are recorded. The 16-ton smack barge *Ellen* was launched in 1874 for William Burley of Newham, where there was a quay at the end of the short goods railway line from Truro. By 1885, *Ellen* had been sold to a Plymouth owner. In October 1876 Trethowan launched the 99-ton (later registered at 109 tons), 26m-long schooner *Flora* for Bisson and Dawe of Penryn, for use in the lucrative transportation of cattle from Spain to Penryn. On 28 October the *Royal Cornwall Gazette* reported the launch of this vessel, but erroneously gave the name as *Bushman*, of 200 tons burden. This name never appears in official records. The 200 tons could be an estimated weight of cargo *Flora* could carry. J.H. Wellington, the shipwright up to then employed by Trethowan, was given as builder, although only the latter's name was recorded in the official registers.

The wharf area is under the care of the National Trust; the old stone quay, probably dating back to Daniell's time, is still substantially intact. Its wall is pierced at intervals by sloping apertures; four being over 4m wide, one of 3m, and a larger at 8½m. The latter may have been widened by Trethowan for use as a slipway at high water. The others are thought to be copper ore shutes for loading vessels when moored at low water. Timber shutes probably assisted this process.

Next to Roundwood lies the small tidal Cowlands Creek. On a narrow strip of foreshore at the end of the creek in 1872 J.H. Wellington, Trethowan's shipwright, built the small 60-ton schooner *WRT* for his own use. In 1875 William Burley, recipient of the barge *Ellen*, decided to go into shipbuilding on his own account. Also on Cowlands Creek, probably on the same site as *WRT's* build. Burley built the bigger 84-ton schooner *William and John*, launching her in May 1876, also for his own use. His enterprise came to nought for she was wrecked off County Wexford the following year.

In the early twentieth century the Scoble family of Malpas operated a coalyard at Roundwood and with the growth of leisure activities on the Fal hired out pleasure boats and ran a tea garden. In 1944 pleasure was not the first priority of the hundreds of US Army and Admiralty personnel involved in secret preparations for D-Day. The deep narrow waterways and sheltering woods of Tolverne and Turnaware were ideal for hiding and preparing the landing craft destined for the Normandy beaches. Access roads and slipways built by local construction firms still exist. The Smugglers Cottage became an administrative centre, and there must have been much traffic along the Fal between there and the similar preparations in Falmouth.

Roundwood Quay from Halwyn, December 2005. Lamouth Creek extends top right and Cowlands Creek bottom right..

During the last century the deep waters of the Fal have been used extensively for the laying-up of redundant ships, sometimes of considerable size, during times of trade depression. Visiting tourists on the Falmouth passenger launches or crossing on the King Harry Ferry have been amazed at the sight of the vessels from all parts of the world tethered to massive buoys within the narrow wooded confines of Tolverne. The number of ships has risen to eighty or more at a time over the whole of the estuary, including the Penryn River, King Harry Reach, Tolverne, Malpas and even the Tresillian River, where they dried out at low water. There were large numbers of merchant ships during the hungry 1930s, post-war redundant fighting ships of the Royal Navy, and tankers during the 1950s oil shortages. Men from the hamlet of Coombe, tucked within the delightful Cowlands Creek, at times were employed as watch-keepers on groups of ships which were tiered up together. An important part of the job was to shepherd some of the skeleton crews back from the local pub late at night and pour them into the punt alongside the King Harry Ferry Quay. On rowing them back to the ship the boatman had to ensure they could climb the boarding ladder!

At the time of writing only one small ship lies in Tolverne Pool. During the summer months the river is alive with commercial tripper boats, canoes, motoring launches and yachts. Not many yachtsmen bother with the challege of trying to sail in these confined waters as their predecessors had to. In the winter the river is left to the birds, apart from the occasional puntsman oyster dredging. Formerly the men of Coombe would supplement their income by setting their 'perches' of oyster beds out of the main navigation channel, marking them with withy rods and dredging the oysters when they had grown to size.

Tolverne Pool from Roundwood Quay, December 2005.

From Tolverne the River Fal reaches towards the east, separating from the main shipping channel to Truro. Great sand bars, bare at low water, extend across the entrance, but a channel is navigable for a small yacht for a kilometre or so at high water. Drop an anchor here on a summer's day and you could be in a remote tributary of the Amazon, with absolute silence and tranquillity apart from the singing of birds in the tree-clad hillsides and the splash of rising fish. But don't daydream too long: the sluggish ebbing tide will suck the water from beneath your keel and you will be surrounded by acres of mud for half a day. Before rising sea levels and centuries of tin and china clay workings filled the upper rivers with mud it is believed that small ships could reach a wharf at Tregony, nearly 6km from Tolverne. Now it is only possible for small dinghies to go half that distance to Ruan Lanihorne on a good tide. So the river is mainly left to itself: in the winter the untroubled haunt of little egrets, grey heron, kingfishers, and a variety of migrant wading birds and ducks, find ample feeding amongst the salt marshes and rocky shore-line.

The main navigation channel heads north from Tolverne, with hillsides of mixed arable and dairy farmland to port and the woodland of Lord Falmouth's vast Tregothnan Estate on the starboard hand. Towards Malpas the channel becomes shallower, with mud banks exposed at low water. Here the channel again divides: to starboard the creek heads for Tresillian, 4km away. It winds through woods and farmland, in places over 300m wide, giving an indication of the Ice Age forces which originally carved it. Today the tide has to fight its way upstream over the mud which is solid from bank to bank, apart from the stream which cuts a meandering channel. The last barge-load of roadstone was taken to Tresillian Quay in the 1950s; today only a rowing boat might make it on a good tide.

Malpas lies on the north bank at the junction of the Truro and Tresillian Rivers. It is surrounded by rich agricultural land, with views across to valley-sides clothed in ornamental and natural woodland. There is some residential development here now, but the settlement once consisted of no more than a waterman's inn and the cottages of families of fishermen, bargemen and a ferryman. Footpaths and bridleways lead down the steep hillsides to ferry crossings which date back to medieval times. The Tregothnan Estate still supports a ferry rowing boat for foot passengers which operates throughout the year apart from Christmas Day or in adverse weather, such as high winds which can funnel through the valley. Over the centuries larger ships coming up on the tide to Truro often discharged their cargo here. Goods would then be carried along the riverside road, or on shallow-drafted lighters to the town quays. As at Restronguet and Penryn, timber would be put overboard and rafted up to timber ponds in the shallower areas below the town. Today Truro-bound passengers on the Fal pleasure boats are still often landed at the Malpas stage, just as their predecessors disembarked from steam launches in Victorian times. Today the journey continues by bus rather than horse-drawn carriage.

There was once a shipyard close to the landing stage, the site now occupied by creek-side development. This was the yard of Scoble & Davies, who mostly built schooners for Truro merchants investing in typical voyages to Newfoundland, South America and Europe, or coal and iron cargoes from South Wales. Vessels included the 123-ton schooner *Jesse*, launched in 1866 for Coad & Co., eventually lost in Carmarthen Bay thirteen years later. *Village Belle,* a 137-ton schooner of 1875, was built for R.S. Hitchens, having ten years

View of the mansion and estate of Tregothnan, the ancient seat of the Boscawen family, published by Twycross in 1846. This lithograph by Greenwood captures the grandeur of the scenery and depicts examples of vessels which made their way to Malpas and Truro at the time. (Cornwall County Record Office PD/485.)

Two small 'inside' barges wait for the tide at Tresillian. (RCPS.)

of service before being lost. *Janie*, an almost identical schooner, was built for Hitchens the following year. Greenhill states that the trade of these vessels included triangular voyages to Newfoundland, from thence to Brazil with salted cod, and then down to the Rio Grande for hides; returning to Plymouth or London. In 1877 the 73-ton schooner *Flora*, having the same name as Trethowan's earlier vessel, was also built for Hitchens. Another schooner of similar dimensions to Scoble's *Flora* was built at the yard the following year. This was *Henrietta*, also registered at Truro, unusually having a long career of about fifty years and converted to ketch rig by 1926.

The shipwrights' largest vessel was the 180-ton brigantine *Malpas Belle*, built in 1872 for R.S. Hitchens of Truro. Under various owners she sailed as far as South America in fifty years of trading. However in 1880, by then with a third mast added, her career was nearly cut short. On 18 December the *Falmouth Packet* newspaper reported her arrival off the Lizard following an encounter with an Atlantic hurricane en route from New York with a cargo of maize. Crew member twenty-one-year-old Sam Libby from Polperro was lost when knocked overboard by the foresail and the vessel had been thrown onto her beam ends. After a thirty-four-day crossing *Malpas Belle* limped into Falmouth minus her fore-topmast, with sails split and bulwarks washed away. In the *Mercantile Navy List* of 1910 she was called a barquentine, although *Lloyd's Register* perversely called her a three-masted brigantine or schooner. By 1918 she was Manchester-owned and in 1921 registered in Guernsey. In February 1922 she was caught in a gale while carrying bog iron ore from Antwerp to Penarth and driven onto the beach at Seaton, South Devon, where she went to pieces.

Two barques, possibly timber ships from Scandinavia, lie at anchor at Malpas in the late nineteenth century. (RCPS.)

Richard Skinner Hitchens seems to have been a very successful and wealthy man to have been able to purchase so many vessels in a short time. However, the *Harrods Directory* of 1878 lists his profession as broker and commission agent as well as ship owner. He may have sold vessels on or organised the participation of local speculators in acquiring shares in vessels or cargoes. Merchant vessels could be part-owned by many people, their value divided into sixty-four shares, holders owning multiples of '64ths'. The largest shareholder, perhaps having a half or three quarters of the whole, was known and registered as the 'managing owner'. The idea of using 64ths *may* have evolved from mast-making. To turn a squared baulk of timber into a round mast for a large ship, adze-men would trim off the four corners along the length which would result in eight sides; the next corners were trimmed, making sixteen sides. Two more trimmings made sixty-four sides, which were finished off with draw-knife or plane. Regulations governing this share system were laid down under an Act of 1825.

On rounding a bend above Malpas the high ground recedes on either side. The spires of Truro Cathedral, 3km away, come into view across what appears to be, at high water, a vast inland lagoon, part river, part Calenick Creek. However, very close attention must be given to the navigation buoys marking the circuitous channel towards the tidal barrage and Lighterage Quay. Boscawen Park lies on the starboard side; a green oasis set on reclaimed land, with its lower point known as Sunny Corner. Apart from several early records of Truro-built vessels, this is the highest point of the Fal tributaries where a commercial shipyard existed. Charles Dyer set up business here prior to 1870, building a

The demise of *Malpas Belle*,
wrecked on the beach at
Seaton, South Devon. (Bartlett
Library NMMC.)

variety of trading vessels in the next two decades. The 64-ton *Emu* was built in 1870, with
dandy-rig (similar to ketch), for Mitchell Bros, Truro merchants dealing in commodities
such as coal, timber and lime. According to a newspaper report, by 1875 she had been
fitted out as a Corunna to Penryn cattle trader under the ownership of Mead & Mitchell.
Alpha, of 1871, was a 66-ton schooner used in the Newfoundland fish trade, later ketch-
rigged for coastal work. *Ulelia*, a 58-ton schooner launched in 1877, was also used on the
Newfoundland run before she was sold to Appledore owners and also converted to a
ketch. She was lost with all hands off Ireland in 1930. The Truro registered *Carrie* was built
in 1878; she was a larger schooner of 104-tons. *WJC*, built two years later, was another
local schooner later converted to ketch-rig. In contrast to the larger vessels, in 1885 Dyer
completed the 32-ton smack barge *Mystery*.

Lambe and Calenick creeks lie on the port side of the river. Here begins the industrial
and commercial face of Truro. Some of the most successful tin smelting works existed
at Calenick and nearby Newham, helping to make rich merchants such as the Lemons
and Daniells, whose names are perpetuated in the city streets and buildings. The long
-abandoned goods branch line of the Cornwall Railway terminated at Newham Wharf.
As the name suggests, 'new ham' was originally a Saxon settlement, probably pre-dating

The Port of Truro in the late nineteenth century, with the partly built cathedral dominating the town. Timber ponds line the Malpas Road bank while on the Newham side industrial buildings have spread along the river. (RCPS.)

the foundation of Truro. The latter site, however, had more room to expand, was closer to existing overland trade routes, and for a time had the dubious protection of a castle. The Allen and Kenwyn Rivers which unite here into the broader Truro River provided a water supply which could be harnessed for many domestic and industrial purposes. They thereby assisted the settlement to develop into a market town which was given borough status in the twelfth century. Even though it is 15km from the open sea it became one of the principal ports of the South West, controlling the whole of the Fal Estuary except the Penryn River and the area later taken over by the upstart port of Falmouth.

The establishment of the mid-nineteenth-century rail network and later improvements to the road system brought a gradual decline in Truro's maritime affairs. Nevertheless, at the end of the century the city's wharves and river channels were still busy with small steamers and sailing barges, well illustrated by the photographs in Peter Gilson's book *The Upper Fal*. During the twentieth century there was almost the complete destruction of the city's maritime heritage. The tidal quays, which for centuries had enabled vessels to tie up right in the heart of the city, were filled in and built over, the two rivers either culverted or hidden behind high walls. The port's commercial buildings, grain elevators, flour mills, and warehouses, have either been demolished or converted to riverside apartments and offices.

The port was not yet dead. In 1939 it could still boast of handling 57,000 tons of imports, that amount nearly doubling in 1944 during the Second World War. In the second half of the century, although trade was a fraction of those figures, at the new facility at Lighterage Quay at Newham vessels still brought in bulk commodities such as coal, sand, roadstone, ore concentrates, grain, fertilizer and calcified seaweed. The harbour authority is still committed to keeping the navigation channel open, dredging being carried out when necessary. In 2005 the main import was cement from Bremen and other continental ports. Twenty-one shipments arrived, the largest being 1,400 tons. Scrap iron was exported in the opposite direction. The port can handle vessels of up to 85m in length

A grassy island sits in the middle of the River Allen channel below the stone-built Boscawen Bridge, completed in 1862. This replaced an earlier timber structure of 1848. The building of bridges hastened the development of Truro and the infilling of the river channels and ancient quays. The schooner on the mud-bank on the right dwarfs barge *Daisy* at the quay. (RCPS.)

with a draft of 4m at mean high water. Visiting yachtsmen, with smallish boats, and if they are brave enough to negotiate the channel, may tie up by the Harbour Master's office somewhere beyond a vast supermarket and car park, which the planners thought suitable for a prominent riverside setting in Cornwall's Cathedral City.

FOUR

THE BAR AND HARBOUR SHIPYARDS

THE BLUETT AND SYMONS FAMILIES

In April 1801 Nelson battered the Danes into submission at the Battle of Copenhagen, by August returning down-channel after refitting the fleet to harry the French at Boulogne, where Napoleon Bonaparte's shipwrights were building, needlessly it turned out, a fleet of barges to invade England. Constant war, population increase and inefficient methods of land management were causing food shortages and escalating prices throughout the country. In Cornwall the poor were starving: miners and their womenfolk marched to towns, rioting and threatening merchants, so that eventually there was legislation to regulate prices. The local situation was relieved to a degree by the arrival in Falmouth of imports from America: in March, merchants William Hambly & Co. were expecting about 1,000 barrels of superfine American flour, '….the discharging any part of the said cargo in Falmouth, will depend entirely on the quantity that can be disposed of in the neighbourhood.' In April, Hambly's were also selling 400 barrels of Virginian flour, arrived in the brig *Lucy*; and in May George Croker Fox & Sons were to auction about 1,800 barrels of wheaten flour and Indian meal, shipped on the *Matilda* from Philadelphia. Not to be out-done, in June, merchant Joseph Banfield advertised for sale bags of Indian corn, and barrels of flour, pork and beef, which had arrived on the brig *James*. For a day at least, the local shipwrights were able to take the minds of the local population off their troubles. On 25 July the *Royal Cornwall Gazette* newspaper announced:

Two new packets will be launched at Falmouth on Monday evening next: the *Earl Spencer*, from the yard of Mr Bluett, to be commanded by Captain Cotesworth, and the *Duke of Kent*, from that of Messrs Symonds, for Captain Lawrence. This will be a very pleasing sight, as they will both go off perhaps at the same moment, and being within a very small distance of each other, may be both viewed from the same spot.

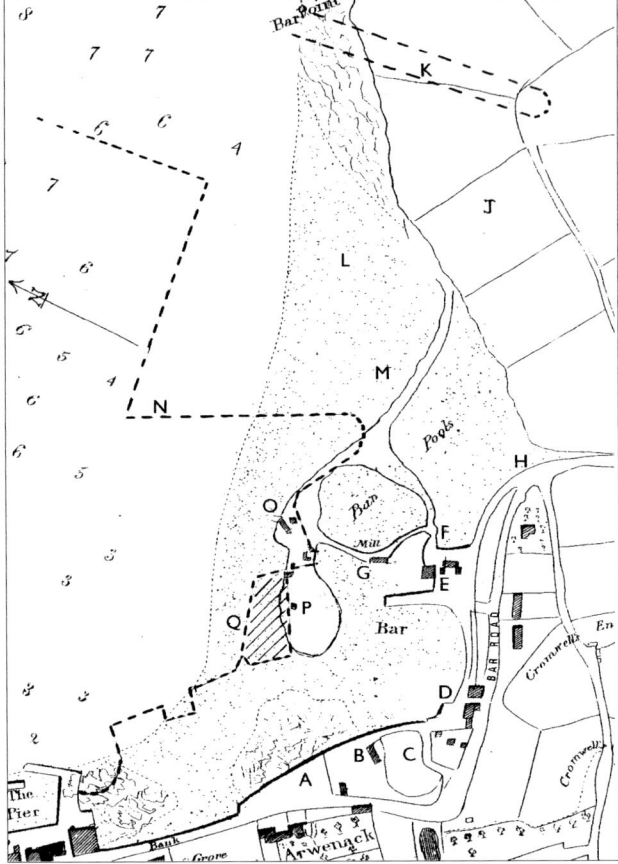

THE BAR. Site Location Plan (superimposed on R. Thomas's map of Falmouth, 1827).

The occupants are listed in chronological order, see text for approximate dates. The dotted line represents the modern shorelines. Falmouth Docks extend over and beyond the upper half of the map. The Killigrew Monument, Bar Road, and the Docks railway station may be used as reference points when comparing with the Ordnance Survey Map.

A	Killigrew Monument.
B	Trethowan's Yard, R.E. Barracks, Territorial Army Centre, car park.
C	Timber Pond, parade ground, car park.
D	Manor Yard: Crouch, Wilmore, Mayn, Pope?, Broad, Haley?, Burt, Thomas.
E	Bar House (later entitled the Dock Inn, Dock and Railway Hotel, Riviera Hotel, Admiral Nelson) W.H. Lean's shipyard and jetty.
F	Banfield/Trudgeon mill.
G	Netherton's (Bar) Mill (located within the eastern half of the Port Pendennis marina pool).
H	Railway Cottages.
J	Docks railway station
K	Queen Elizabeth Dock
L	Cox & Co's foundry.
M	Lean's outer shipyard.
N	County Wharf.
O	Burt's shipyard.
P	Symons, Harvey's yard.
Q	National Maritime Museum, Cornwall.

Shipwrights and apprentices, believed to be at Porthleven, posing at a typical small boat-building yard in the early twentieth century. (Bartlett Library, NMMC.)

According to *Lloyd's List*, the registered tonnage of *Earl Spencer* was 206 tons, and *Duke of Kent* 180 tons. An enthusiastic and colourful report of the event appeared the following week:

> The launch of two new ships at this place on Monday last for the service of the Post-Office drew together a vast concourse of people from the neighbouring towns and country. The sight was delightfully picturesque. The beautiful variety of scenery, groves, hayfields, houses, ships, and water sprinkled with innumerable boats, all grouped together, and all crowded with spectators – heightened by the music of the Royal Cornwall Band, and the cheers of the multitude, as the ships glided majestically into the water; formed a treat highly gratifying to the beholders.

Richard Bluett, Gent., married Sarah Lovell on 27 December 1764; a male heir, by tradition being given his father's name, was born in 1773. Unfortunately this Richard died when only seven years old, and the next male child, James, born fifteen months after Richard, became heir. To muddy the waters further, or perhaps on reflection to clear them, a later boy, born in 1781, also received the name of Richard. It seems likely that it was this Richard who, according to Susan E. Gay, became a Post Captain in the Royal Navy. James was only seventeen when in 1791 his father died. The following year Sarah Bluett and her son James were responsible for the lease of the Bar mills, and, by

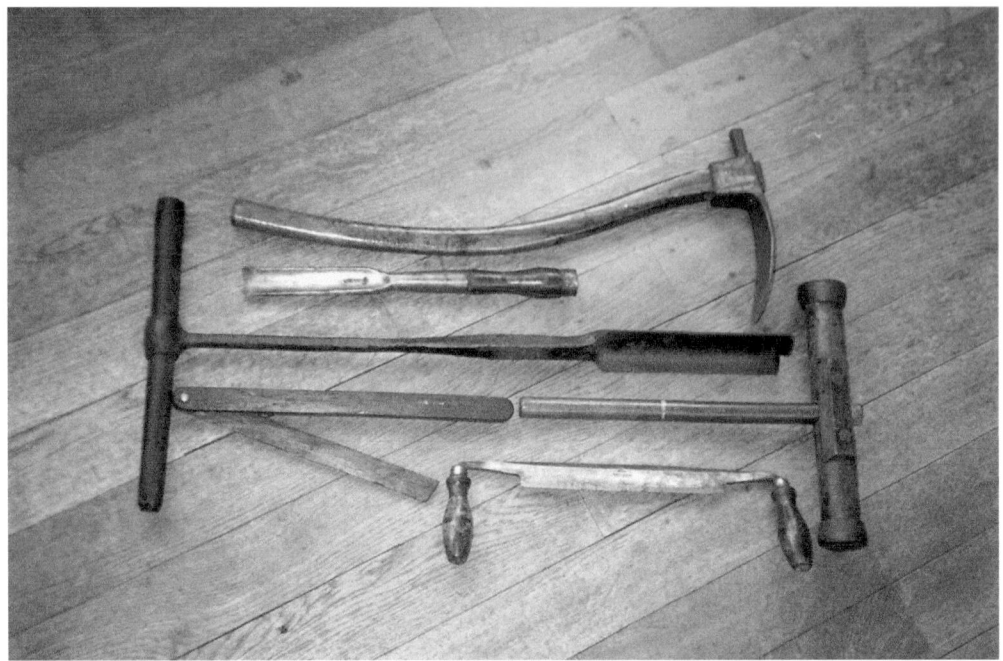

Shipwrights' tools. Items include an adze (top) with which a skilled man could work rough timber to the required shape; chisel; auger for boring holes for treenails and bolts; bevel for checking the angle of frames; caulking mallet; and draw-knife for finishing masts and so on. (Exhibits in the National Maritime Museum, Cornwall.)

implication, their shipyard. However, in 1799 *The Universal British Directory* still listed the yard under the name of the deceased Richard Bluett. Son James may have been serving an apprenticeship there, and, considering the scale of work carried out in the next few years, certainly needed to employ a large team of highly skilled shipwrights.

Sarah Bluett may not have been in good health at this time, and was to pass away in April 1803, aged sixty-two. James was certainly in control of the yard, when only six months after the launch of the *Earl Spencer*, and with what must have been frantic activity at times, the *Royal Cornwall Gazette* on the 6 February 1802 reported: 'On Thursday evening a fine new ship of 400 tons was launched from the yard of Mr Bluett… The launch was a very fine one; and the ship is considered one of the completest and largest ever built in this harbour.' The vessel was the *Ives*, ship-rigged, 98ft (30m) in length and officially registered at 258 tons (the 400 tons was probably the estimated carrying capacity). She went first to London owners and then to Bristol, being sold elsewhere in 1808. It was a pity that the weather was bad and the hour late, for there were few spectators to the spectacle of the launch, for this was the dramatic finale to the Bluett yard. On 24 April that same year the following advertisement appeared in the *Royal Cornwall Gazette*:

FOR SALE BY AUCTION,

On MONDAY the 17ᵗʰ Day of May next, by two
o'Clock in the Afternoon, and the following days
till the whole is disposed of; at Mr BLUETT's,
Ship-wrights-yard at the Bar, Falmouth,

THE STOCK IN TRADE, of himself and partner; consisting
of a quantity of Oak, Fir and Elm, PLANK and TIMBER;
Spars and Mast Pieces, Deck Deals, the FRAMES of two
VESSELS, one of about 100 and the other of 40 Tons
measurement; a number of new and second-hand **BOATS,**
and a **SCHOONER** completely fitted out, about 28 Ft
long; a large quantity of Oars and Handspikes, Brown Okum,
Pitch, Tar and Rosin, a large assortment of Nails, Paints, Oil,
&c. and a variety of other Articles belonging to the said
Business of a Shipwright, all which will be put up in small Lots
for the convenience of the Purchasers.

The whole may be viewed the week before the Sale, and further
particulars known, by applying to **JAMES BLUETT**, at the Bar;
or to
L. HINGSTON, Auctioneer Falmouth.
Falmouth, 22ⁿᵈ April, 1802.

From the mid-eighteenth century a number of packet vessels and naval brigs were built
by Peter Symons, said to have been followed by his son Richard, at the Little Falmouth
yard, adjacent to Flushing village and where later (1820), a dry-dock was constructed. On
Richard's death in 1837, this yard passed to his son Thomas. However, it may have been
two of his relations, John and Robert Symons, who were in charge of a yard on the Bar
by 1801. The press reports quoted above seem to make clear that the two packet ships
were launched in this instance from the Bar, and not Little Falmouth. That yard was a
nautical mile away from Mr Bluett's yard on the Bar. As the launchings were −'within a
small distance of each other, (and) may be both viewed from the same spot' the 'Messrs
Symonds yard' must have been that of John and Robert, who were already established on
the Bar, having built the ship *Walsingham* in 1794.

In October 1811 the 180-ton packet brig *Montague* was launched from Mr Symons'
yard at Little Falmouth. The following August a very similar brig, the *Lady Mary Pelham*,
left the slipway of J. & R. Symons' yard on the Bar. The *Montague* was equipped for the
service with sixteen guns and the '*Pelham* about fourteen, with complements estimated
at forty crew each. The following year both vessels were involved in one of the most
dramatic episodes in the history of the Post Office packet service. On 14 October 1813 the
Pelham sailed from Falmouth for Brazil; four days later she was followed by the *Montague*.
According to letters and reports later received, both packets arrived at Madeira on about

30 October. Notwithstanding that a large hostile American privateer schooner, the *Globe*, lay off the island, they continued the transatlantic voyage. The *Globe* caught up with them about ninety miles to the west the following afternoon and commenced firing on the *Montague*, which replied vigorously. The schooner had a superior force of over eighty men and her ship's guns and small-arms fire caused death or injury to half of *Montague*'s crew. Nevertheless, inspired by Captain Watkins, who fought on although seriously wounded by a musket ball, his crew twice repulsed boarding parties. Their guns inflicted so much damage on *Globe*'s hull that she began taking on water.

A Board of Inquiry was later brought because of accusations that the *'Pelham* apparently took little action until two hours had passed, when she closed with the *Globe* and gave her a broadside which at last caused her to withdraw in a shattered condition. Eventually evidence proved that the *Pelham*'s Master was following earlier instructions by Commander Norway on *Montague*, who was killed in the battle. The two brigs sailed back eastwards to Tenerife for repairs and later *Pelham* continued to Brazil. *Montague*, which had sunk the mails at the height of battle, made her way homeward. She did not arrive in Falmouth until 5 March 1814, when the *Cornwall Gazette* newspaper reported that she had come in under jury masts from Scilly, where she had been on shore and received much damage. Captain Stevens brought *Pelham* in on 19 March, apparently after no further encounters with privateers.

The *Montague* was taken to Little Falmouth for extensive repairs. An advertisement appeared in the *Cornwall Gazette* of 7 May for the sale at Flushing and the Little Falmouth shipyard of equipment from the brig. It indicates that she was to be almost completely re-rigged and fitted out, the proceeds of the sale probably going to the estate of the late Commander Norway. The sale list included sails and yards, part of the main mast, standing and running rigging, 'the whole which was new about twelve months since, but damaged by shot.' After a shake-down cruise in July to Bordeaux and back, on 9 August Captain Watkins sailed with the mails for Jamaica. He was still Master in 1826 when *Montague* was last recorded in *Lloyd's Register*. In 1815 the *Lady Mary Pelham* had the misfortune to be captured by the *Kemp*, another American privateer, but was rescued soon afterwards. Her misfortunes may have been a reason why she left the packet service in 1816 and thereafter traded out of Falmouth as a merchantman. She was replaced in the packet service by a larger Thames-built vessel of the same name.

According to returns made to the Admiralty by South West shipyards in 1804, the Symons yards in Falmouth were by far the biggest employers apart from a Mr Tanner in Dartmouth, South Devon. Richard Symons in Little Falmouth employed forty-five shipwrights and eleven apprentices; J. & R. Symons and Co. seventeen shipwrights and twelve apprentices. (Also on the Fal, four yards in St Mawes, those of Lane, Hawkins, Roberts and Jennings, employed a total of thirty-five; and Richard Dingle in Penryn employed nine.) In 1815 John and Robert Symons launched the 22-ton sailing barge *William and Alfred* for Broad & Co., but by 1823 *Pigot's Directory* is listing Francis Symons as shipwright at 'Arwinnick yard' on the Bar. The family connection with John and Robert has not been found. Robert had drowned one stormy night in October 1821 when he fell off the northern arm of the Custom House Quay. By the 1841 Tithe listing Francis controls the whole Bar area and two early houses and gardens on what became Bar Crescent were held by the executors of John and Robert Symons.

The Thames-built 198-ton packet brig *Lady Mary Pelham* at Malta in 1818, being the second packet of that name. The first, a similar vessel of 180 tons, was launched at the Bar by J.& R. Symons in August 1812. She was replaced by the depicted vessel after clashes with privateers but continued as an English merchantman under Falmouth registration until about 1824. (Copyright NMM Cornwall.)

A lithograph by George Rowe, around 1861, depicting the outer Bar from the Pendennis end. The curving stone revetment towards Symons' yard represents work done to consolidate the bank for shipyard use. Both Lean and Burt were to establish yards here. The small yawl-rigged boat on the beach appears to be a very early example of a Falmouth quay punt. (Falmouth Art Gallery.)

In 1810 Francis S. Symons appears as a shipping agent: in an advertisement in the *West Briton* in October that year, interested parties are asked to apply to him regarding booking a passage to Lisbon on the *Pheasant*, a twelve gun private Ship of War, with thirty-five crew commanded by John Quiller. She had accommodation for twelve passengers and storage for bullion and 50 tons of goods. Two months later, Symons of Falmouth also advertised the auction of the hull of the 84-ton ketch *Dulwich*, with all gear. A few number of records of the output from the yard run by Francis have come to light. In 1821 he launched the 232-ton barque-rigged packet *Prince Regent*, followed in 1827 by the 50-ton sloop *Cordelia* and the 87-ton schooner *Falmouth*; other vessels included the 128-ton brig *Achor*, 1831; the 66-ton schooner *Sylph*, 1836; and in 1840 the 213-ton barque *Edward Hayes*. (The brig depicted by Thomas Allen on the 1831 engraving could be the *Achor*!) In 1841, competing in the building of the type of craft being turned out by Trethowan nearby, he built the pilot cutter *Alliance*. She had the small dimensions of the early types: 44ft (13.40m) in length and nearly 7ft (2.1m) in depth, registered at 22 tons. Apart from wooden screw steam tugs in later years, such as *Carbon, St Keverne, Dida*, and *Chough*, little else is known of the firm's production. Francis Symons, shipbuilder, is listed in *Pigot's Directory* for 1823 and 1830, and *Robson's* of 1840, where he is still advertising his lodging house and baths already mentioned in the chapter on mills. In the 1841 census he is listed with wife Cordelia and three daughters. It seems that his son, whose birth is noted eleven years earlier, had not survived (unless the newspaper had the sex wrong). However, from about 1856 the directories list the firm as Francis Symons & Son. This was George, who later took over the business.

After the Bluetts the Symons family probably operated the two yards at the Bar; Arwenack or Manor Yard within the creek, and the other on the outer Bar. The latter is depicted on the Farington and Allen engravings, with buildings and ships on the blocks. The Richard Thomas Falmouth map of 1827 and the Tithe map do not agree regarding the position of the buildings, which, being constructed of timber, as requirements changed were not permanent structures. A number of larger, more substantial sheds had been erected by the 1860s. The firm advertised in *Warne's Directory* of 1864 as shipwrights, mast and spar makers and shipsmiths; 'always in stock' was ironwork, timber, masts and spars, oak, elm, and pine plank; plus oakum, pitch, tar and varnish. In 1878 one of the last vessels, if not *the* last, to be launched by George Symons was *Gwendolyn*, a feminine name for a big powerful 67ft (20m) cutter which drew nearly 10ft (3.0m), as much as a schooner of similar length. She was built for local tailor R. Toms as one of a number of highly competitive cruising outfitter vessels, supplying shore-going clothes to British and Continental sailors arriving back in home waters. *Gwendolyn* was re-registered in Dartmouth in 1883 but later returned to Falmouth, being sold to a French buyer in 1918.

Curiously, the 1880 Ordnance Survey map marks the Bar site as 'Timber yard', although the lease transferring 'Symons Shipwrights yard' (then occupied by George Symons) to Harvey & Co. of Hayle, who established it as a timber yard, was not issued until 1887. Photographs appear to show that Harveys rebuilt the large sheds, which became a local landmark because of the firm's name written large on a roof. Other ancillary buildings appeared on the site, including 'Bar Yard Cottage', which housed the yard foreman. Harvey & Co. carried on through two world wars as the adjacent dockyard developed and the Bar

Overlooking the Manor Yard, pre-1890. Sailing vessels lie in the Town quay beyond the Killigrew Monument on the left. A schooner is at Symons' Quay at the entrance to Bar Creek. The hulk and small craft are on Trethowan's slipway. The number of vessels in the harbour is astonishing. (RCPS.)

pools gradually filled with rubble. Over the years parts of the foreshore of the outer Bar were built up and revetted with timber or stone quay walls. One part in particular, facing towards the Killigrew Monument, in the 1920s was still known as Symons Quay. The area saw much activity during the Second World War: Harvey's sheds sheltered stores for the United States Army, who constructed concrete slips for landing craft in preparation for the 'D-Day' invasion of France.

THE TRETHOWANS

We proceed by trying to describe the other Bar shipyards, or something of the business of their occupants, in an anti-clockwise direction as they were located along the foreshore of the main Bar pool, or creek as it was sometimes known, and along which Bar Road properties were developed. John Trethowan's yard, possibly founded in the same decade as that of Francis Symons, was situated on the Arwenack shore, on the north side of the enclosed timber pond, within a stone's throw of the manor house. Its long rectangular shed, end-on to the beach, is clearly seen on the Tithe map and Richard Thomas's map of 1827. The Wodehouse Estate conveyance of 1848 lists Trethowan's property as a timber pond, shipwrights yard, sawpits, buildings, slips and sheds. His covered sawpit once existed on The Green, the area in front of Arwenack House which is now the town car park, dominated by the Killigrew monument.

Between about 1832 and 1864 John Trethowan produced small schooners such as the 54-ton *Jane and Mary* in 1842 for the Mediterranean trade. He also built the smaller type of local craft at the Bar yard, including pilot cutters and quay punts. Trethowan produced the 22-ton *Victoria* (cutter No.7) for T. & E. Chard in 1837; she was eventually wrecked on the Manacles in 1851. Chard replaced her the following year by another Trethowan boat, registered with the same name and number, but, at 32 tons, a third larger. Cutter *Prince Albert* was also built for Chard in 1841. The yard launched *Harriet* in 1844: the *Register* gives her dimensions as 46ft (14m) long, 13ft (4m) wide, and nearly 8ft (2.4m) in depth, a craft of considerable width and depth, with great stability and sea-keeping qualities. *Water Nymph* was completed in the same year for Pope & Co. of Falmouth. The registers list P. Pope & Co., 1858-66 (see *Arrow*), and E.C. Pope as owners in the 1880s. She was condemned in 1887. (Also see Pope under Mayn's yard below.)

The 23-ton, 37ft (11.3m) cutter *New Providence* was launched in 1841 for pilot J. Vincent, probably to replace an earlier *Providence*. A few years later she was sold to St Ives owners, and in the 1850s underwent a metamorphosis when rebuilt as a 55 ft (17.0m) 32-ton schooner. Under this new guise she had a remarkably long life as a trading vessel. From 1874, back under Falmouth registration, she was owned by the Nicholls family of Gerrans and based at Portscatho. A decade later they sold her to the Beer family, master mariners, shipbuilders and merchants of West Pembrokeshire. The Beers originated in Cornwall, Thomas Beer having built their schooner *Three Brothers* in Truro in 1841. According to an article by John Beer[1], *New Providence* worked from small harbours in the Newport (Pembs.) and Milford Haven area for forty years. She carried cargoes such as farm produce, coal, bricks and timber to and from western ports from Cornwall to Merseyside. A photograph taking during repairs to her hull in about 1885 shows that she may have then been ketch-rigged, her name and 'Falmouth' as port of registration are prominent on her square counter stern. *New Providence*'s logbook ended in February 1922 when she was laid up in Sandy Haven Creek near Milford. She became a picturesque wreck, sketched by artists such as Graham Sutherland.

The nineteenth-century sailing cutters varied in size, one of the largest, at nearly 70ft (21m), being No.6, *Arrow*, built by John Trethowan in 1863. The final bill still exists[2]: detailing the cost of everything including hull, spars, paint, ballast, rigging, leather, grease, and even spy glasses and binoculars. The accountants' final bill totalled £810 6s 1d: it was issued on 31 December 1863 in Falmouth by Philip Pope, who seems to have been a major shareholder. *Arrow* is sometimes recorded as being built in the Little Falmouth yard, leased by John in 1851, but in the Bar is a possibility. John's son, Henry Stevens Trethowan, expanded the business, having been assigned the lease of the Little Falmouth yard in 1865. He became the largest employer in the area. Many fine schooners and even larger vessels were produced at the new yard, and also at Roundwood Quay, on the upper reaches of the Fal. The Bar yard was similarly involved in repairing or fitting out craft such as schooners and brigantines.

Although Henry Trethowan was acknowledged as an excellent shipbuilder, he was certainly not a businessman. Perhaps his reputation had drawn him into taking on too much work, for in 1876 the business crashed. A small bundle of solicitors' letters and reports in the County Record Office reveal a huge list of people to whom he owed money, many being suppliers of shipyard materials[3]. There was a meeting of creditors on 28 July: assets had been estimated at £7,796, whereas liabilities were over £20,000.

The Little Falmouth shipyard, 2005. The site of the birth of packet ships and and merchant vessels.

A faded but unique photograph of shipwrights, some posing with caulking mallets and adzes, alongside a large vessel, believed to be in the Little Falmouth dry dock. (RCPS.)

(Another report stated that he owed the bank £10,000 and other creditors £14,000.) The outcome was that his affairs were to be settled by liquidation and handed over to trustees. The assets included his house, sheds, sawmill, gridirons and such at Little Falmouth; sheds, boats and materials at the Bar, Roundwood Quay, and the Victoria yard on Falmouth High Street. He also owned shares in the pilot cutter *Alarm*, and most of the shares in the Trieste-built 420-ton trading barque *Giovani*. The vessels then in various stages of construction at Little Falmouth were a barque of 'East India outfit', with copper-sheathed hull, a large schooner, also sheathed, and two fishing smacks. At Roundwood Quay there was a schooner of 200 tons burthen, and at the Bar a similar schooner, with 'Baltic outfit', and a fishing smack. (A vessel of East India build was of superior quality to the Baltic, and though more costly received better *Lloyd's* classification.)

The Roundwood Quay vessel was the *Flora*, discussed in the section on the Upper Fal. The large schooner at Little Falmouth was the yacht *Governor Cairns* of about 125 tons, for the government of Queensland, eventually launched in November. One of the fishing smacks was presumably the 70-ton dandy-rigged *Mystery*, registered in Grimsby on the East Coast. She had a relatively long life for a fishing boat, but was eventually lost when stranded on the Schelde Estuary in Holland in 1906. Some of Henry Trethowan's work was featured in Basil Greenhill's famous *The Merchant Schooners* (1951) where he stated that 'All the work was done by hand; there was never a machine in the (Little Falmouth) yard…' However, the legal proceedings concerning Henry's bankruptcy, and a report of a dispute regarding the *Giovani* and his yacht *Glendoveer* brought before the County Court[4] reveal a different state of affairs. Improvements made to the property since the lease was assigned to him by Mr Symons included 'a steam saw mill, an engine, and certain other machinery'.

How the bankruptcy was resolved is not known, however. H.S. Trethowan, at the Bar, is still listed in the *Kelly's Directory* up until 1893, although the area was leased by the War Department from the Kimberley Estate in 1889. Here barracks were built for a volunteer division of the Royal Engineers, and a special unit for servicing a harbour defence scheme of electronically detonated mines laid on the seabed between Pendennis and St Anthony. In 1890 a 122m-long iron pier had been built from the shore near the Killigrew Monument to accommodate a special mine-laying barge. A light railway went from the barracks to the end of the pier on which there were small cranes. This structure was not removed until the 1970s, when it was still referred to as the submarine pier. In the 1920s the barracks became the local headquarters of the Territorial Army. The buildings were demolished in the 1990s and the site has recently been redeveloped as a car park.

THE MANOR YARD

We move along Bar Road to the site of the lime kiln and yard which in the 1840s was operated by William Crouch & Sons. This was one of a number of kilns located around the Fal and adjacent coasts, near to the shoreline so that ships could discharge their cargoes of limestone close to them. In *Warne's Directory* of 1864, Crouch advertised as corn, flour, salt and general merchants, commission agents, importers of fruit and foreign

Bar Creek from the mill dam, high tide, *c*.1900. On the left are W.H. Lean's sheds and jetty, the latter by this time derelict. On the extreme right small craft lie on Harvey's inner beach. To the left of the obelisk the Royal Engineers' barracks occupy Trethowan's yard. (Royal Institution of Cornwall.)

produce, having offices in Church Street, with stores at the Bar. By the 1880s Arthur Wilmore had supply stores here, and R.A. Newcombe was proprietor of the lime kiln. The lime burner was Sampson H. Pascoe, who lived in the adjacent cottage, not the healthiest of places to reside.

Referring back to the Tithe map – the next property towards the Bar House area was probably once Bluett's yard, later occupied by James Mayn, who appears in the directories from 1830 to 1856. Mayn had obviously been operating there prior to 1830; an advertisement appeared in the *Falmouth Packet* in April 1830 for the auction of the fast sailing smack *Kitty and Clara*. She was of the Port of Falmouth, about 20 tons, and offered with stores and materials. She was to be auctioned at Mr J. Mayn's shipwright's yard near the Bar, where she was lying on the beach, recommended for the coasting trade or as a trawler. Some examples of the output from Mayn's yard are *Gem*, pilot cutter number four, of 29 tons, built for John Chard in 1845, and *Wasp*, No.13 for J. Lowry. Both these families lived in cottages close by Falmouth parish church. Mayn also built schooners, in 1840 the 50-ton *Ellen* for Tillas & Co., trading to Portugal, and in 1845 the 59-ton *Blue Bell* for his own company, for the Mediterranean trade. In 1848 he launched the *Gazelle:* she was registered at 94 tons, and had dimensions of nearly 68ft (20m) in length, 18ft (5.5m) beam, and 10.6ft (3.25m) draught. It is recorded that Mayn operated her to St Michaels on the Azores, most likely on the fruit-carrying trade. He sold the schooner to Pope & Co. in 1861, and ownership passed to J. Trigg in 1864. Sadly, she was lost in the Mediterranean the following year.

A trawl through early editions of the *Falmouth Packet* has revealed only one further craft to represent the output from Mayn's yard, the schooner *Queen of the Chase*. She was built by Mayn in 1852 and registered at 79 tons; ten years later being lengthened and upgraded

A placid harbour scene in the early twentieth century. Schooners and steam-powered cargo vessels lie at anchor in Carrick Roads. Nearer are graceful yawl-rigged yachts and quay punts, a number of which were probably built on the Bar. (RCPS.)

to 98 tons. She was initially owned by Pope & Co. of Falmouth. Several firms with similar titles have been traced, either one in the same or perhaps family related. A contemporary account published in the booklet *Port Navas* states that Pope & Co. operated fast fruit and general cargo vessels to the Mediterranean and Newfoundland. An Edward Colin Pope, sail maker at the Quay, was listed in the 1856 *Post Office Directory*, comtemporary with the building of the ship. Another contender is J.H. Pope & Co., who appear in *Kelly's* in 1873 as shipbuilders at an unknown location on the Bar. They also had premises as chandlers and merchants at 31 Arwenack Street. The 1883 edition of *Lloyd's List* gives Edwin Pope of Wood Lane, Falmouth owning two Ipswich-built schooners, the 144-ton *Enchantress*, and 123-ton *Forest Fairy*; also the Bridport 145-ton Brigantine *Red Rose*. In 1905 *Queen of the Chase* was over fifty years old, a remarkable age for a coasting schooner, from 1881 owned and skippered by Sydney Bate, originally from Port Navas and later residing at Beacon Terrace, Falmouth. In April, Bate left Cardiff bound for Plymouth with a cargo of coal; his crew of four included two of his sons. They beat down as far as Lundy Island, where adverse winds compelled Bate to run back to Cardiff, where that night he dropped anchor in the roadstead. The Bristol Channel has one of the highest tidal ranges in the world. While trying to improve position to a more secure anchorage the schooner went aground and capsized; the wind strength was only force two. The five crew were rescued and cared for by the local Shipwrecked Mariners Society.

According to the Tithe map, the property adjoining Mayn's yard was held by William Broad & Sons, probably as warehousing. Broad & Sons, in parallel with the Fox family, were for many years prominent merchants, shipping agents and vice-consuls. They owned their own ships and handled sales of imported cargoes, which included anything from Welsh iron to hogsheads of port and sherry from Portugal and Spain. They also dealt with the sale of wrecks, such as in February 1895 when representatives travelled to

Porthoustock to dispose of the remains of the 1,965-ton sailing ship *Andola* of Liverpool. She had been carrying a cargo of wheat from Tacoma, Washington, on the Pacific seaboard of the United States. After an arduous voyage, which included rounding Cape Horn, *Andola* anchored in Falmouth Bay, probably waiting for orders and re-provisioning; a welcome break for the crew. Her intended destination was Hull, but as experienced mariners know, the English Channel can at times be more deadly than Cape Horn. From the newspaper report it seems that the ship left Falmouth and proceeded up-channel, but soon encountered a stiff north easterly wind. She tacked towards the French coast and back again towards Cornwall, and may have been trying to get back to Falmouth. In fact she had been driven backwards; blinded by snow squalls she went aground on the Manacles and began to break up. Fortunately the disaster was seen from the shore, and the Porthoustock lifeboat managed to save all twenty-eight crew, who were taken to the Royal Cornwall Sailors Home in Falmouth. Broad's auction of the wreck included sailcloth, yards, copper and hatches, plus 'useful wood for farmers and others'.

Following from Mayn at the Manor Yard (called 'Arwenack yard', presumably the same place) came shipwright Benjamin Blamey, working there from 1856 to at least 1867. In August that year he advertised for sale the 235-ton barque *Selena*; she had been built in Newcastle in 1856 for the Brazilian trade. Most shipyards competed to obtain brokerage business for ship sales, which may have incorporated lucrative refitting work prior to the sale. The same month his neighbour, W.H. Lean, was selling the larger Sunderland-built barque *British Queen*. In 1863 Blamey built the 62-ton coasting schooner *Waterlily*, which in 1871 was sold to Captain W. Bunt of Port Navas on the Helford River. Later she was skippered by his son-in-law Sydney Bate, and possibly ketch-rigged. Part of his journal (extracts in the book *The Story of Port Navas*), describes often hazardous but otherwise successful voyages around the British coast. (See also *Queen of the Chase*.) Also on the Bar during the same period were ship-smiths Dunstone and Blamey, and also shipwrights John and Joseph Haley. The latter pair may have been predecessors at Lean's yard nearby. In 1852 Joseph Haly built Pilot Cutter No.1, *Harriet*, of 31 tons, for Vincent of St Mawes, and No.2 *Andrews* for Messrs Andrew in 1857, 'a beautiful vessel, and reflects much credit to the builder.' The Manor Yard was extended over the years with the construction of slips, gridirons, quays and sheds.

The available directories list Charles Burt & Co. at this yard in the 1890s, but the firm had already been here for some years. The *Falmouth Packet* of 20 September 1879 reported that a fine cutter (the *Ida*) had been launched from Mr Burt's yard in Falmouth, intended for Mr Sampson Hicks' outfitting trade. Hicks was a well-known tailor, one of several established in the town. A profitable trade had been developed by some tailors, who sailed out on hired boats or in their own craft, fast cutters similar to the pilot boats, to meet incoming ships. They faced the same dangers as pilots and quay puntsmen in trying to outwit their competitors to reach their quarry first. If invited on board by the Master they then offered to supply new shore-going suits – after a very cursory measuring – to sailors who may have lived and worked in the same salt-stained clothes for the previous one hundred days or so. Hicks was successful enough in the business that by 1898 he could afford to move into the substantial villa of Number 1, Bar Terrace, a later residence of the Burt family. Larger craft were built at Manor Yard. In 1883 Burt launched the 87

The Manor Yard, *c.*1920. Low tide in the creek. Eddy Thomas, his son Bert and shipwrights stand on a carpet of wood shavings amid the products of their trade. (RCPS.)

-ton, 103 ft. (31m) wood-built steam tug *Armine*, and in August the following year the 80 ft (24m) ketch *Irene* for Gray & Son of Penryn. Burt was said to have launched a new vessel almost yearly for the previous nine years.

WILLIAM EDWARD THOMAS

The Burts appear to have given up this site in about 1900 to concentrate on their yard on the outer Bar. They were replaced at the Manor Yard by William Edward ('Eddy') Thomas, who had earlier run a successful, but inconveniently located, yard on the south side of Bar Road, near the junction with Avenue Road and opposite to Trevethan's yard. Craft to be launched had to be hauled across Bar Road and down a long slip into Bar Creek, a distance of about 100m. An astonishing report in the *Falmouth and Penryn Weekly Times* on 10 December 1892 highlights the expertise and sheer determination of the small workforce, and the amazing craft they were capable of creating:

LAUNCH OF A SALVAGE STEAMER AT FALMOUTH. – There was successfully launched at Falmouth on Monday evening, a salvage steamer, built by Mr W.E. Thomas for Mr A.G. Anderson, diver and salvage contractor, of Falmouth and Liverpool. The steamer is remarkably strongly built, and though only 95 ft. long, 18 ft. beam and 9 ft. in depth, she weighed without machinery, nearly 150 tons. She was built at least 120 or 130 yards from the water's edge, and the task of launching was unusually difficult, and altogether occupied more than a week. The vessel had to be got across the main road leading to the railway station, which was blocked for many hours, during which all vehicular traffic had to be diverted. Having been got across the road, some delay was caused by the vessel running off the ways, but she eventually took to the water in a splendid manner. The steamer is to be engined immediately by Cox and Son, Falmouth. The engines will be of the compound surface-condensing type, and of great power. The vessel will carry an 8-inch and a 12-inch centrifugal pump, which will be capable of delivering 3,500 gallons per minute. Forward there will be a powerful steam winch and a heavy casting on the bow for lifting heavy weights. The steamer has one watertight iron compartment, and will be able to carry about 8 tons of fresh water stored in galvanised tanks for supplying the boiler. The steamer, which is to be fitted with the electric light, and have electric submarine lights, is to be named the Etna, and is expected to attain a speed of 12 knots.

In May 1895 *Etna*, complete with all diving equipment, was auctioned at the town quay by Messrs Rowe & Corlyon, and bought by J.H. Hunt for £610.

Recently found copies of indentures establish that, confusingly, there were two William Edward Thomas's, the first 'Eddy' becoming apprentice shipwright to John Trethowan in 1848. He in turn took his son Eddy under his wing as an apprentice at his own yard in 1874. It is impossible to know when one replaced the other in charge of the business. The Thomas's were best known for building wooden working craft such as quay punts, sometimes collaborating with Burt on designs for fast yacht punts for the highly competitive regattas and for leisure sailing. He is said to have designed the first of the type, *Pride of the Port*, in 1879 (see description under Quay Punts). However, comparable craft, perhaps smaller, must have already been in use for 'bum boat' work. Also in 1879, Thomas is said to have made another punt as a speculation, which was seen by the well-known author of books on yacht design, Dixon Kemp, who suggested that it would have made a good yacht. It was fitted out as such by Thomas, who, in 1880, helped the new owner, a Welsh yachtsman, to sail it to Cardigan Bay via Milford Haven. After a successful racing season there, it was named *Wonderful*. This was the first of many such conversions and custom-built craft. Another Thomas punt is *Sophie*, which was launched in 1892. She seems to have been worked and raced before being converted to a cruising cutter-rigged yacht in 1912. Under various owners she has sailed the South Coast and Solent ever since and at present is undergoing restoration on the Hamble. Several others are still actively sailed with the original yawl rig in the West Country.

By 1902 Thomas had taken over from Burt at the Manor Yard, his ex-neighbours on the newly built Bar Terrace no doubt pleased that the earlier sound of the hammering of rivets close at hand had now ceased. Part of his old yard became cab-proprietor Aaron Smith's stables, and by 1912 Marine Crescent had been built over the site. Thomas handled a great variety of work at the Manor Yard, including conversions of the quay punts into yachts. As ships calling at Falmouth became fewer, the puntsmen fitted auxiliary engines or sold off their sailing craft and ordered larger motor-powered work boats. At least two were built by Thomas in the early 1920s for the Morrisons and others. The 38ft-long *Elsie*

Watercolour painting of the Manor Yard, around 1922, by Charles Hugh Thomas. (Bartlett Library NMMC.)

Watercolour of the launch of a motor cruiser at the Manor Yard, around 1922, by Charles Hugh Thomas. (Bartlett Library NMMC.)

was built for Walter Morrison and installed with a 40hp engine. He and his son used it for fishing, pleasure and charter trips, and even tug-work.

The Manor Yard is depicted in its heyday in amateur watercolour paintings by the young Charles Hugh Thomas, possibly Eddy's nephew, who served an apprenticeship at the yard from 1920. They are now of significant historical value, and were fortunately shown to the curator of the Falmouth Maritime Museum some years ago by a Mr Farndon, who allowed them to be photographed. They depict a substantial boat-building shed and workshops, a jetty revetted with timber piles, and a wide slipway leading up from the beach. One yacht or quay punt sits in a mud berth, and others are pulled up on the slip on which the men are apparently adzing a baulk of timber into a mast or keel. Hulks of two wooden ships dominate the beach towards the Submarine Pier, possibly being coal hulks careened for cleaning and re-caulking, as described by Douglas Robinson in his delightful book *Bar Pool*. Another painting records the ceremonial launching of a large motor cruiser, which is dressed overall. Bar Terrace and its gardens fills in the background.

Even though the inner mill pools were being filled in at this time, Bar Creek was still a natural tidal inlet. Schooners came in at high tide to unload timber for Harveys, and even the well-known Thames sprit-sail barge *Lady Daphne* was seen unloading cement at the old Symons Quay at the end of the outer Bar. Craft of all kinds were on out-hauls or beaching legs, perhaps waiting for a buyer or repairs. One of the more unusual semi-permanent fixtures was the old brigantine *Julie*, from Nantes in France, owned by the artist Henry Scott Tuke and used as a studio. Tuke was a resident in Falmouth for many years, taking an active part in the local yachting scene. He competed in many regattas in various yachts, including *Red Heart*, *Flamingo* and *Flame*. Many of Tuke's most famous paintings were maritime scenes around the port and on board the *Julie*. A number also featured naked boys, one model being a lad employed at Thomas's yard, who, according to Douglas Robinson, received a good deal of banter from his friends. No doubt one of these was Bertram Charles Thomas, who became an apprentice in his father's yard in May 1916, not knowing that in 1926, not long after he was due to complete his seven years, the yards would be closed and the creek turned to stone rubble.

By 1927 Eddy Thomas had re-established the business at a new yard at the western end of North Parade at Turnpike Creek, Ponsharden, on the Penryn River. It is believed that Eddy soon retired, and the building and repairing of yachts and motor boats was carried out by his brother Tom and son Bertram (Bert). By 1935 Bert was advertising himself as yacht builder from his home in Wodehouse Terrace. The Turnpike Creek yard carried the name of W.E. Thomas into post-war times, but under the ownership of Silley, Cox & Co., but possibly managed by Cyril Thomas. During the Second World War Bert Thomas, and many others, used their family legacies of shipwright skills to help the war effort. This seems the appropriate place to highlight the work of the Falmouth Boat Construction Company.

At around the outbreak of war, this company took over an area of the waterfront behind Falmouth High Street. Access from the road was obtained via ancient steep narrow opes (pronounced 'opp'). Part of the area, Briton's yard, had been cleared of a number of stone tenement cottages in 1936, the residents being re-housed by the town

Tuke's brigantine *Julie* moored to the mill dam, around 1885, at a time when the mill building was reasonably intact. (Royal Institution of Cornwall.)

council. This area, with its slipway, an old packet warehouse, and the entertainment venue Malin's Hall (which still exists) at 39 High Street, comprised the new yard. In these cramped conditions, twenty-four powerful motor launches, torpedo boats and the like, up to 34m long, were built for the Royal Navy. The double-diagonal mahogany ply hulls were manufactured and sent by road in kit form from Brentford, Middlesex. Fitting out was carried out at the Ponsharden shipyard and at the warehouse jetties of the shipping company of Coast Lines at Boyers Cellars. (The site of old pilchard processing works on the south side of Turnpike Creek.)

Several hundred workers were employed along that waterfront during the war, mainly local men skilled in a variety of marine trades, ably supported by about two dozen local girls employed as 'mates' to painters and other tradesmen. At Coast Lines wharf, two girls Ada Dunstan and Mary Rich, *née* Penver, ran a canteen above Admiralty offices in one warehouse, cooking daily for up to one hundred workers. In an adjacent building armourers serviced guns, depth charges and torpedoes for the flotillas of fast Fairmile motor launches and RAF rescue boats based outside on the jetty. Newly-built craft from the High Street yards were towed round for Packard engines to be installed at Ponsharden, where an old dry-dock had been re-commissioned. Painting and fitting out was carried out alongside the Coast Lines' jetties. On the shore next to Turnpike Creek a barrage balloon unit provided some protection from low-level air attack. The enemy bombs, which caused damage and death in Falmouth, fortunately missed this sensitive area, the only major scare occurring when an RAF launch on the jetty blew up. Fortunately it was towed clear and beached across the river before it could devastate the whole area.

Above: Shipyards, Falmouth, a sketch by Henry Rushbury, R.A., 1957. The view from an upper window in the High Street. Merchant vessels are in the docks, and the harbour tug fleet lies off the waterfront. Malin's Hall is to the right and the supposed packet warehouse to the left. Between lie the sheds of the Falmouth Boat Construction Company. (Bartlett Library NMMC.)

Right: Celebrations at 39 High Street in July 1965, prior to the launch of a new yacht built by the Falmouth Boat Construction Company, emulating scenes which must have occurred here when naval launches were completed during the Second World War. (D.Graham.)

An example of a Fairmile 'D' Royal Navy motor torpedo boat under later Royal Air Force livery.
Vessels such as this were built at 39 High Street, Falmouth and fitted out at Ponsharden.
(John Mitchell.)

In late March 1942 from here sailed the flotilla of sixteen motor launches, brought together from various coastal bases, to accompany HMS *Campbeltown* on 'Operation Chariot', the heroic raid on St Nazaire. As the crews and commando units gathered in Falmouth prior to sailing, the people at Ponsharden worked to prepare the boats. These had to be re-painted in a non-reflective drab mauve colour known as 'Plymouth pink'. Extra fuel tank and Lewis gun and Oerlikon cannon deck mountings had to be made and fitted at short notice. Attempts were made to provide some upper-works protection to the otherwise vulnerable teak and mahogany hulled craft, unfortunately to little avail, as very few, nor their crews, returned home.

WILLIAM HENRY LEAN

One can only guess at the changes which took place during the nineteenth century around the old Bar House. However, from the available records and maps the historical sequence may have proceeded thus: in about 1820 Symons constructed a long timber jetty out into the creek in front of the Bar House, and possibly erected another building to improve facilities for his lodging house and bathing enterprises. Later, Symons himself, or another shipwright such as Benjamin Blamey, erected sheds on the jetty and on the shore next to the neighbouring Manor Yard. By 1862, with the addition of slipways and a steam engine house, this had became the shipyard of W.H. Lean who soon gained a reputation for building excellent merchant schooners and ketches. A typical example, when first built, was the schooner *Little Reaper*, launched in 1863; 77ft (23.5m) in length and registered at 80 tons. She was owned for at least ten years by Burnett & Co. of Falmouth; within that period what appears to have been almost a complete rebuild was carried out. She was lengthened to nearly 96ft (29m), a third mast was added, and she was

Coast Lines' former sheds and jetty on the Penryn River, 2006. The marina now occupying Turnpike Creek lies beyond.

re-registered at 108 tons. By the 1880s she was owned by James Pritchard of Runcorn in Cheshire. Throughout her career many voyages were made to Newfoundland in the long- established cod fish trade. She was finally wrecked on the Smalls, off the western tip of Pembrokeshire, in March 1891.

A Lean ship with a particularly long history was the 76-ton *Wild Wave*, launched in 1873 as a ketch for Laudy of Dublin. She was a few feet shorter than *Little Reaper*, the *Register* notes that she was partly iron-bolted, which may have extended her life. In 1904 she was re-rigged as a schooner, and in 1926, probably because of her age, her allowed tonnage was reduced to 58-tons. She disappears from the list in 1940, after spending all her sixty-seven years apparently in the hands of Irish owners and Masters. Another large ketch was launched in about 1874, one of many specially fitted out for the shipment of cattle from Corunna in Spain. For about twenty-five years in the latter half of the century, Spanish cattle were shipped over, in cargoes of about sixty at a time, and off-loaded at ports such as Plymouth and Penryn, as part of government contracts to feed the armed forces and for commercial sale. Although steps were obviously taken to keep the stock on board in good condition, the procedure was undoubtedly cruel, especially when adverse winds lengthened voyages. In April 1881 Penryn merchants Bisson and Dawe's schooner *Flora* was driven off course, ending up in Ilfracombe after thirteen days at sea. There was very little fodder or water left for the sixty cattle below decks. This practice came to an end not long afterwards due to public pressure from bodies such as the Church Society for the Promotion of Kindness of Animals. Another example of Lean's output at this time is the 61ft (18.60m) tailor's cutter *Francis*, built in 1878 for outfitter S. Jacob. This was a slightly smaller craft than *Gwendolyn* which was being constructed the same year at George Symons' yard nearby. There must have been considerable rivalry and speculation between apprentices as to which cutter was to be the best.

Apart from giving employment to a great number of local men, Lean served on the town council, he was a Justice of the Peace, and became Mayor in 1874. In 1879 he was president of the Town and Quay Regatta, and in his yacht *Spinaway* successfully competed in the 10-ton class on many occasions. Business interests were varied, including using the yard for marine sales, such as in May 1879, when salvage goods, including boilers, cannon, winches, timber and tools from the SS *Stromboli*, wrecked on the Lizard, were auctioned there. The yard also produced fine quay punts, and in the 1880s, in spite of a serious fire, a number of wood-built, steam-powered tugs came off the blocks, including *Pendennis*, *Defiance* and *WJ*. In 1885, following the example set by Emanuel Martin at Ponsharden (Chapter 3), Lean built the big (97 ton) wooden ketch *WHL*. Under Falmouth registration she was initially operated by Lean and then T.J. Gibbon, before being transferred to a Belfast owner. She was last recorded in 1918 under Guernsey ownership. In 1889, also in wood, came the passenger steamer *Falmouth Castle*, in which Lean used an engine built in his foundry a few years earlier. Also in the 1880s Lean began leasing part of the outer Bar, parts of the old mill pools, by now filled in, and the old foreshore raised with rubble from the dock excavations. It is not known when the yard by the Bar House – by then the Dock and Railway Hotel – was abandoned. Perhaps both yards worked in tandem, wooden vessels were built at the old, and steel at the new site. Douglas Robinson, in *Bar Pool*, indicates that it was out of use by 1922.

The passenger tug *Princess Victoria*, built by Cox & Co. in 1907 It is crowded with day-trippers on a winter outing, as it tows a laden schooner, believed to be Lean's *Mary Barrow*, past Malpas bound for Truro. (RCPS.)

W.H. Lean's beautiful clipper-bowed, steel-built *C & F Nurse*, probably the last merchant sailing ship to be built on the Bar. Her sails may be patched but they are setting well as she leaves Falmouth on the starboard tack. (National Maritime Museum, Greenwich.)

Lloyd's List gives W.H. Lean as operating the 273-ton barquentine *Anne Duncan* for several years from 1879, and the 84-ton Danish schooner *Union* for a decade from the same year. In the 1890s Lean owned several trading schooners, one being the Falmouth registered 74-ton *Maria Elizabeth* (launch date and builder not known), which he had purchased after 1890 from P.J. Brown of Devoran. In January 1895, while carrying granite from Penryn to Bristol, she was caught in a south-easterly gale and blinding snow in the Bristol Channel. Forced to try to get into Padstow as she was leaking badly, she went aground below the awesome Stepper Point. A dramatic and successful rescue of the four crew ensued, involving five Trinity pilots residing at Hawkers Cove, and the Breeches Bouy Rocket Brigade. The resultant sale of the wreck realised ten shillings!

The well-known 164-ton three-masted topsail schooner *Mary Barrow* took to the water in 1891. She spent some years in the Newfoundland cod trade and voyaging to South America, before returning to British coastal waters in 1905. Here she carried China clay northwards for the Potteries, returning with coal from the Runcorn collieries, to be discharged perhaps at Falmouth or Truro. She is featured in several photographs, including one depicting the perils faced by sailing ships. This was taken after a January storm in 1908, after she had been driven, in company with the similar vessel, *Lizzie R. Wilce*, high up on the beach at St Ives. She was eventually refloated with little damage. The *Lizzie*, built in 1876 by local shipwright John Stephens at Yard Point on Restronguet Creek for the West Indies fruit trade, was not so fortunate and ended up as a coal hulk. *Mary Barrow's* luck ran out in 1938, when during a gale in the Irish Sea she was wrecked on the Calf of Man. Unlike the work of Cox & Co., shipwrights at the adjacent docks, there is little known of the steel vessels launched by Lean. Exceptions are the 62-ton tug *Britannia*, which in 1893 cost £2,800 and was fitted out for trawling as well as tug work. She was initially sold to a Swansea owner for work in the Bristol Channel, but later also saw service in London and Brazil.

Lean's experience with merchant sailing vessels, combined with the yard's expertise in working with the comparatively new material, drew at least two orders for large steel schooners. The resulting beautiful craft were something of an anomaly at a time when most potential buyers were rejecting sail in favour of steam-powered vessels. The three-masted 165-ton *Victoria* was launched in February 1897. She was 105ft (32m) long and nearly 23ft (7m) wide, but with a comparatively shallow draft of 10.6ft (3.2m). She had been ordered by E.O. Roberts of Liverpool, but by 1916 was owned by W. Gould & Son of Barnstable. She was sunk in April the following year, it is believed by a German submarine. The 117-ton, 27½m *C & F Nurse* was built in 1900 for owners F. & C. Nurse of Bridgewater, Somerset, who operated her from the Severn mainly for coastal trading. The last owner was Kelly in 1927. Her career came to an ignominious end in 1936: according to Greenhill she became a storage hulk at Sharpness on the banks of the Severn.

Mr Lean died in the winter of 1899, a glowing obituary appearing in the *Cornish Echo* on 31 March. The business was then taken over by his nephew, confusingly also called William Henry Lean, who having worked in his uncle's yard for many years, carried on in his footsteps. He also served on the town council, was a keen yachtsman, and as a member of the Royal Cornwall Yacht Club, officiated at regattas and sailed his uncle's *Spinaway* to further successes. Sadly, only fourteen years later, at the age of fifty, the second William

R.S. Burt's boatyard on the outer Bar. Harvey's sheds are to the right. (RCPS.)

A beautiful half-model of a quay punt, originally made to facilitate the construction of the full vessel at a Bar shipyard. (Exhibit in the National Maritime Museum, Cornwall.)

Henry died, leaving a widow and four children. It is not known if the business survived his death for long; the palmy days of sailing quay punts and craftsmen-built steel schooners was coming to an end. This was 1913, and the eve of the First World War: the area was busy with the expansion of Falmouth Docks, which were soon to be taken over by the War Department. Shipwrights skilled in wood, iron and steel would be needed there.

RICHARD STEVENS BURT

The firm of Charles Burt & Co., which has already been noted, built craft at the Manor Yard from the 1870s to about 1900, also leased part of the outer Bar, which had been owned from 1860 by the docks company. Here, next to Harvey's timber yard, Burt built sheds and a quay. When Charles retired, his son Richard Stevens took over; his business card comprehensively read 'R.S. Burt & Son, ship, yacht, launch and boat builders, smiths and motor engineers, marine surveyors and valuers, contractors to the Admiralty, War Office, RAF. Telegrams to Burt, Docks, Falmouth'. The card also noted that Falmouth quay punt type yachts were a speciality.

R.S. Burt must have built and repaired a great variety of craft of which no records survive. However, the plans of a few have been deposited in the Bartlett Library. Some of the names and descriptions of the punts have been passed down through word of mouth and in the regatta reports in local newspapers. Most importantly, some craft still exist, or some at least survived for many years. Probably the most well known of Burt's 32ft (9.75m) class is *I.C.U.*, which, with Walter Morrison at the helm, often crossed the line ahead of the fleet. In January 1905 she was sunk and was badly damaged in collision with the local tug *Penguin*. A few days later with the assistance of a steamer and diver she was raised and beached by Burt's yard. After extensive repairs, by September she was winning races again. For proof of Burt's boat-building skills one can look no further than this craft. After the First World War, Mr Morrison sold *I.C.U.* to a salvage firm, who copper-sheathed her and shipped her out for salvage work on the coast of West Africa. Many years later, in the 1960s, she somehow turned up in Northern Australia and was used by a firm of pearl divers. She was lost on a reef in 1988.

The shorter 28ft (8.5m) *Curlew*, built for Frank Jose, was launched in July 1905, winning at her first two regattas the following month. For over thirty years Mr Jose used this boat for quay punting, fishing and racing. Inevitably, after the First World War there was a rapid decline in the number of visiting ships needing the service of the quay punts, and those still working were fitted with engines. *Curlew* was one of a number of working boats converted to yachts. She had a number of owners and modifications before being found in poor condition in Malta in 1968 by Tim and Pauline Carr. They undertook a major refit and for twenty years sailed the world in her, for much of the time minus an engine, reaching Newfoundland, South America and Australia, to name but a few. Their last major cruise was to Antarctica, and for some years *Curlew* found a berth in South Georgia. Eventually she was returned to Falmouth, this time on a cargo vessel, and is now often on display at the National Maritime Museum, Cornwall. She is berthed within a few metres of where she was built, a tangible monument to the memory of the shipwrights of the Bar.

In the 1920s, with the post-war revival of leisure pursuits, the yachting community recognised the speed, stability and sea-keeping qualities of the craft, and yards began to build new quay punt yachts to the customer's requirements. One of the most impressive built by Burt, practically at the end of boat-building on the Bar, was the luxurious 24-ton auxiliary yawl *Diana*, launched with great ceremony in June 1926. She was designed by Burt for General Sir Frederick Poole of Cotswold House, Fowey. The craft had dimensions of 43ft (13m) in length, 12ft (3.7m) in beam, and 8ft (2.4m) draught.

Quay punt *I.C.U.* in serious working rig surges across the Inner Harbour. The gaff bends under the weight of the hard-sheeted mainsail, but there is a problem with the gaff jaws which are adrift from the mast. (RCPS.)

Quay punts in summer racing rig, one believed to be *I.C.U.* They have set an incredible amount of canvas to goose-wing on the down-wind leg of the course, including a boomed-out spinnaker and an extra-large gaff mizzen. The sail-changing when rounding the mark would be a sight to behold! (RCPS.)

Construction consisted of an elm keel, incorporating a 6-ton moulded iron keel, oak posts and frames, planking of elm below the water and pitch pine above. Decks were teak with laid Colonial spruce. Needless to say, the interior accommodation was lavish. The sail area was 1,690sq.ft. At the ceremony attended by local dignitaries was T. Grose, the yacht's new skipper employed by the General. Much repair and restoration work was also carried out by Burt's men including, in 1923, the re-rigging of the tea clipper *Cutty Sark*, based in the harbour for a number of years.

With the expansion of Falmouth Docks in the late 1920s, R.S. Burt had to relocate his business on the Bar. The trade directories for 1930 and 1935 place him at Little Falmouth, next to Flushing village, but apparently after financial problems he was to lose this yard and probably retired. Previously his brother, W.J. Burt, had been running the Ponsharden Shipyard on the Penryn River, a workforce said to be of up to 170 breaking up or repairing vessels. He died in 1929 but his son Ernest John took over. That site was later sold by the family and by 1933, under the title of E.J. Burt & Co. Ltd, Ernest was building small sailing craft at the Victoria yard below Falmouth High Street. In that year he obtained a lease of part of the rocky foreshore to build two slips. In 1939 the Victoria yard behind the 'Star and Garter' pub was listed as occupied by the Falmouth Yacht & Boat Building Co., possibly managed by Burt. From 1942 to the end of the war that firm had a contract to produce little else but naval whalers. These were general-purpose craft which could obviously be used as lifeboats on ships at sea. They were built in pairs, each pair taking about six weeks (an estimate from memories of sixty years ago), 8m in length, of elm clinker planking, and fitted with drop keels. When completed with two masts and lug sails, they were towed round to Falmouth Docks for probable transportation to Plymouth naval base. Across the river at the Little Falmouth yard the firm were kept busy repairing whalers and other craft which had been in service.

E.J. Burt died in 1964: his son Ron had served his apprenticeship at the shipyard and worked there until the 1960s. He then became a yacht repairer, surveyor and broker with offices at the Victoria yard. A Turnpike Creek lease had previously been obtained by the Burt family, and in 1970 Ron Burt sold it to the Quandrant Marine Company for the controversial development of Falmouth Marina. Post-war the nearby Ponsharden yard had a succession of occupants; Falmouth Boat Construction continued there into the 1960s, followed by small firms including Falcraft Ltd. From 1970-77 the Dredge & Marine Company built steel vessels such as the King Harry Ferry and in the 1980s Riverside Fabrications built tugs and fishing boats. Cockwells Ltd have now revived traditional wooden boat building on the site with the construction of vessels such as the Fal passenger boat and a pilot cutter.

THE FALMOUTH DOCKS

The history of Falmouth Docks has yet to be written. However, as their construction, and the inevitable 'march of progress' eventually led to the complete obliteration of the Bar, a short summary is necessary. The loss of the Post Office packet service in 1850, and the resultant unemployment, brought calls for docks to be built to encourage trade, and therefore employment, by providing safe wharfage and repair facilities for large merchant ships. There

A lithograph by Newman & Co. Falmouth Docks and railway station, *c.*1865. The breakwaters, grain store and two dry docks are shown, but the cranes may indicate that Dock No.1 (the nearest) is not finished. The growth of Falmouth, generated by the railway, is clear by the amount of Victorian development above the old town. (Falmouth Art Gallery.)

A view of the Bar from above the railway station, *c.*1910. Cox's shipbuilding works are to the right and the sheds of Lean's outer yard to their left. Burt's sheds and jetty, with crane, are to the left of the schooner being repaired on the beach. Further left are Harvey's sheds and sawmill. (RCPS.)

were scores of these employed in world-wide trade, passing Falmouth along the English Channel to and from London River and its great Victorian dock system, some of which was still under construction. There was no reason why Falmouth shouldn't try to take a small portion of this trade, or at least have docking facilities available if required. In the mid-nineteenth century there were an astonishing number of craft, from work-a-day ketches to full-rigged ships, and from many nations, calling at Falmouth: a shipping agents' later ledger book for 1881 recorded the arrival of over 200 different craft per month throughout the year. While in port captains paid for services varying from single telegrams (probably informing owners they had arrived in British waters), pilotage and boat fees, bills from local butchers, chandlers and sailmakers, up to major repairs undertaken by shipwrights.

The Act of Parliament for Falmouth Docks to be built was granted in 1859 and a company was formed, the board consisting of a number of local worthies, including shipping agents and merchants. About 150 acres of the rocky foreshore of Pendennis and the fundus (seabed) of the harbour was leased from the Duchy of Cornwall, and in 1860 construction began on the Eastern Breakwater, some 600m to the east of the old Bar area. Dredging of a deep-water channel, and work on the Western Wharf and two graving (dry) docks quickly followed. The completion of this stage in 1863 coincided with the arrival of the Cornwall Railway branch line from Truro. The line carved its way along the slope of the ancient meadows behind the Bar, and terminated at a goods and passenger station conveniently sited near the foot of the Western Wharf. As the docks later expanded, railway lines were laid from the terminus, to the quays and shipbuilding and repair sheds. At this time the harbour was buzzing with activity, very little of it concerned with pleasure. Sailing craft were still dominant, and whether being manned or maintained, were labour intensive. The 1881 census records that out of a population of nearly 13,000 there were 354 mariners and fishermen (some of the former probably in transit), sixty watermen, sixty-one pilots, thirty-four sailmakers and 144 shipwrights. By this time many of the latter would have been employed in the docks.

Rail communication with London and the rest of Britain meant less work for some of the small coasting craft still based on the Fal. Bulk cargoes could now be transferred directly between railway and ships, many of which would soon be powered by steam, moored at the quays. However, apart from tin and copper mining and allied industries, all of which were becoming less viable, Cornwall had no great commercial heartland which would feed substantial income to sustain a trading port. Exports consisted of little more than a few minerals (apart from the expanding china clay trade), fish and granite, much of the latter leaving from wharves at Penryn. Main imports continued to be timber from the Baltic and North America, fertilisers from South America, and grain from as far away as Australia. In 1861 an impressively large stone-built grain storage building was erected, and still exists, near the Eastern Breakwater. Several grain merchants took advantage of this facility including J.M. Goodman who, in 1895, advertised his new steam mills at the docks, proposing that he would grind grain and meals which customers had brought directly from ships at the wharf. This was one of a number of enterprises which rented space from the dock company over the years, including coal and timber merchants and shipbuilding and repair firms, for the early dock company itself was not involved in such enterprises, but leased out its land and infrastructure to others.

The merchant ship *Bedford* in No.2 Dock, around 1870, its steam engines augmented by sail-power. The brick building housed the steam pumping engines to drain the dock. At this time sails, as can be seen in the background, still dominated the harbour. (RCPS.)

A fleet of luggers and smacks arrive in Falmouth to discharge their catch. Before the First World War and subsequent building of dry docks three and four on the area, the beach within the breakwaters was used to land fish which could be carried directly to London by rail. (RCPS.)

SS *Cornubia*, built by W. Gray & Son at West Hartlepool and the second vessel to hold the name, is alongside a wharf in the docks unloading cargo, possibly grain, into Fal 'inside' barges, including *Daisy* of Devoran. The stern view of this barge shows that she is very 'beamy' but is blessed with a graceful transom reminiscent of many Thames sailing barges. *Cornubia* was sunk by a German submarine in the Mediterranean in September 1915. (Royal Institution of Cornwall.)

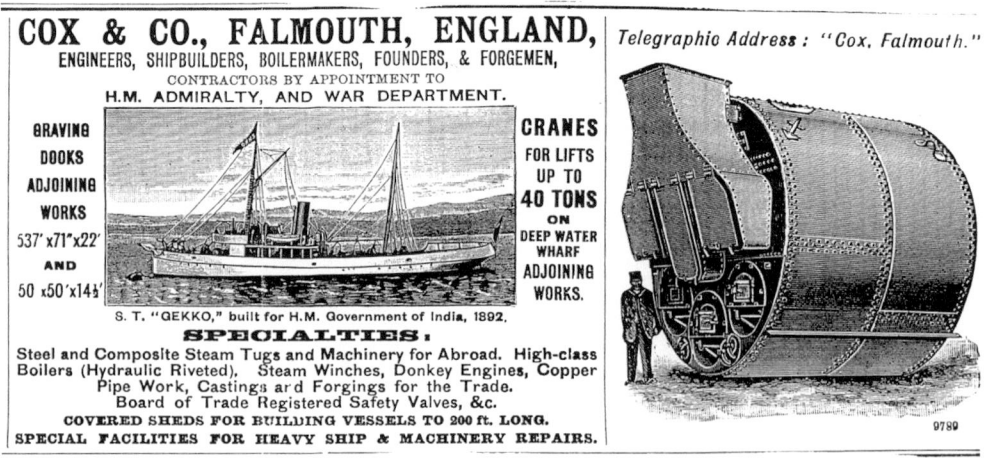

Queen of the Fal, one of Cox & Co.'s many passenger vessels, built for Benney & Co. in 1893. She is crowded with folk in their Sunday best at Market Strand Pier, the approach to the new Prince of Wales Pier, *c.*1906. These vessels and their successors have enabled trippers to enjoy the beauties of the Fal and Cornish coast from Victorian times to the present day. (RCPS.)

Following set-backs, which included storm damage to the new wharves, which were constructed upon massive timber piles driven into the seabed, the company became financially over-stretched; the Public Works Loan Commissioners foreclosed the mortgage and appointed a management committee. Because of Britain's expanding overseas commitments, necessitating at times large naval forces which needed shore-based support, no doubt there was some behind-the-scenes government encouragement to ensure that the project did not fail. It was not until 1914 that the debt was cleared. For the duration of the First World War, the Admiralty became the dock managers, instructing the London company of R.H. Green & Silley Weir Ltd to take over ship repairs. They also imported a large workforce from London. Every crippled ship that was towed in past Black Rock demonstrated the foresight of those who advocated the construction of the docks half a century before. Sheltering in Carrick Roads or Falmouth Bay, iron-clad battleships had now replaced the nation's 'wooden walls' of yore, but the men that crewed them were the counterparts of the heroes of Nelson's day.

In the 1860s the brothers Joseph Goodenough and Herbert Henry Cox were partners in a successful chandlery business based in Arwenack Street near Custom House Quay. At that time the industrial works such as Harveys of Hayle and the Perran Foundry must have been producing skilled metal working and engineering apprentices. It is from a pool of expertise such as this that in 1868, on the west side of the Western Wharf, the Cox brothers developed an iron foundry, smithy and workshops for ship repairs and breaking. From 1878, utilising some adjacent consolidated foreshore, they began the construction of small iron and steel steam-powered craft, under the title of Cox, Farley, and later, Cox & Co. Their impressive 1895 advertisement amply illustrates the firm's capabilities. Until 1930, when shipbuilding ceased, they had built nearly 200 craft, ranging in variety and size from small pleasure launches, local and ocean-going tugs, passenger steamers, naval pinnaces and trawlers. Of the latter, some were the largest of their kind in the world at the time. Other examples of the firm's output are featured in books by Gilson and Kittridge. A smaller company, Pool, Skinner & Williams, built a similar variety of craft at the Dock Head Works in the 1890s, on the area where dry docks number three and four were to be later built.

The Sara & Burgess foundries in Penryn produced a number of powerful steam engines for Cox & Co. They also built several iron vessels on their own account. In December 1879 the *Falmouth Packet* reported the launch of a 65ft (19.8m), fast, 35hp steamer for Falmouth chandler J.H. Deeble, the building of which generated much local opposition because of the noise of riveting. The *Mercantile Navy List* records that Sara built the *Rosetta* in 1880: a 62ft (18.9m), 20hp steam-screw tug also for Deeble. However, without a name recorded for the former and possible inaccuracy of reporting this may be the same vessel. In spite of previous objections to noise from the foundry, in 1881 Sara built the *Udney*, a prestigious 'beautifully modelled steam yacht' for Mr C.E. Treffry of The Castle, Fowey. She was over 18m in length, schooner-rigged, with twin 10hp engines. The deck house over the staterooms was built of teak with plate-glass windows. At the launching in June there was 'great indignation from the concourse (as) Mr Sara has been obliged to refuse many thousands of pounds worth of work owing to a party objecting to the noise of shipbuilding.'

After the First World War Cox & Co. and the docks company were amalgamated, and in the 1920s and 1930s, despite some major economic slumps, there came a steady programme of expansion. In 1924 as many as 1,500 workers were employed. In that decade the first two dry docks were enlarged and two new ones excavated; further wharves were built and, with the increasing use of oil-fired boilers, an oil-fuel bunkering service began. It was during these decades that, at various times, excavated material was trucked in vast quantities on specially laid rails, to be dumped in the ancient Bar pools and creek. Douglas Robinson remembered trains of tip-trucks, which were loaded with excavated rock by steam shovels and hauled by little green saddle-tank locomotives 'with much puffing and panting and blowing of their thin high-noted whistles, pulling them up the relatively steep incline out of the excavations....'

The filling in of the Bar area may not have occurred in the way it did if an earlier scheme had been successful: in 1881 Lord Kimberley had plans drawn up to create a vast dock there, controlled by sea-gates and lined by warehouses; wide quays were to extend all the way round to Custom House Quay. Fortunately this scheme remained on paper. Another much worse environmentally damaging proposal, actively encouraged by the local authorities at the time, was in 1926, whereby a railway was to be built across The Roseland to St Just. Here a major new commercial port was to be blasted out of the rocks midway along the beautiful Fal estuary. Fortunately, for business reasons rather than environmental, it also came to nothing. Falmouth was also spared the sight of the gantries of a container port at the docks, a scheme proposed in the 1980s.

Falmouth Docks and the Bar in 1926. Cox's works and the new graving docks three and four are at the inner end of the Western Breakwater. The whole of the Bar area has been levelled with truck-loads of rubble from the excavations, and Harvey's yard stands alone. (Simmons Aerofilms/RCPS.)

During the Second World War, the people of Falmouth, its harbour and its docks, duly played a major part in the survival of the nation. It is an heroic story which unfortunately cannot be covered here, the painstaking research of others is already in print. From the 1950s there were further extensions to some of the dock wharves, including the construction of County Wharf, which extended on to some of the old Bar area. New roads and railways were laid, and more of the Pendennis rock blasted away to make room for the huge Queen Elizabeth Dock, said to be capable of taking ships of up to 100,000 tons; at peak periods up to 3,000 personnel were employed. It was not always so: during times of recession the docks were almost at a standstill, there were labour disputes and changes of management and ownership.

In 1985 a consortium acquired the yard from the state-owned British Shipbuilders, and now, under the title of A. & P. Falmouth Ltd, from time to time large naval craft, channel ferries, and merchant ships can be seen undergoing repair in the dry docks or lying at the wharves. There is a busy bunkering service, and cruise ships visit regularly. The old number one dry dock is at present the home of Pendennis Shipyard, well known for building a variety of luxury yachts from modern materials. While we admire the magnificent craft they construct, let us not forget the shipwrights of the Bar, who, for three centuries, produced countless craft, from pleasure boats to ships of trade, and let us not forget the men who sailed them.

Bar Road, *c.*1909. The Riviera Hotel is to the left. The timber-built premises shown to its right at this date are the Ladysmith Picnic Rooms; S. Jenkins, grocer; the County Cycle Co., Manager A.E. Belletti; Belletti's photographic shop and motor garage; Doney, Sons & Co., Statuary Masons; T.H. Tresise, general dealer. (RCPS.)

The Admiral Nelson, shortly after its closure in 2005.

Bar Terrace, 2005, once the homes of many employed in maritime Falmouth.

BAR ROAD

The Killigrew Monument, moved to its present site in 1871, and the 'Bar House', recorded as such on early maps, still remain as reference points from which long-lost features can be plotted. The latter was reconstructed or extended on several occasions, and received name changes, from the 'Dock Inn' to the 'Dock and Railway Hotel'. In the early twentieth century as tourist advertising created the 'Cornish Riviera', it became the 'Riviera Hotel', when a new frontage, stables and garage entrance were added. Through the decades, its custom reflected the changes occurring in the nearby docks, the sight of its open doors being sheer bliss to thirsty dockers and sailors, especially in time of war. Reverting for a time after the Second World War to 'The Dock and Railway Hotel', in more recent softer times it received the title of 'Admiral Nelson'. This was not enough to stem its diminishing trade, and it closed in 2004; currently its future is unclear.

From the 1890s, a small linear community, separated from the main town, grew up along the north or creek side of Bar Road. Between the small shipyards there were a few dwellings, interspersed with, at various times, a brewery depot, grocer's shop, monumental masons, plumber, smithy, tobacconist, serpentine works, the Ladysmith Picnic Rooms, several fish curers, coal stores and Belletti's cycle and photographic shops, which, with the changing times, became a motor show-room and garage.

On the other side of the road, perched on the steep slope twixt road and railway, curves the modest but picturesque Victorian row of Bar Terrace. The two first houses on the old meadows opposite Bar House were erected prior to the Tithe survey of 1841, on which one is listed as held by the Executors of Mark Oates; this later evolved into Penwenack

The Bar from the air, 1989. The new marina harbour has been re-excavated across the site of Bar Mill, and houses are being built on the old dock rubble. The Bar House/Admiral Nelson is centre top; the rectangular docks building to the left sits over Banfield's mill pool. Shipyards and commercial premises once lined the curving Bar Road (with Bar Crescent) from the Killigrew Monument, centre right. The new Maritime Museum was later built over what was Harvey's beach, slightly left of the centre. (RCPS.)

Falmouth, docks and town, 2005.

House and the Imperial Hotel. Two adjacent properties were held by the executors of John and Robert Symons, becoming Armyn Villa and Number One, also perhaps Number Two, Bar Terrace. These properties were built on the seventeenth-century 'Cliff', or 'Mill Close' fields once held by Thomas Banfield. In the 1890s W.H. Lean resided at Armyn Villa, from whence he could gaze directly down into his shipwright's yard across the road. From about 1936 Armyn Villa was converted into the 'Sailor's Rest', and is now the Seafarer's Centre, administered by the British and International Sailors Society. Between 1882 and 1893 Bar Terrace was constructed along the road towards the town, terminating at Avenue Road. Many people concerned with the shipyards and docks took up residence, including the Leans, Charles and R.S. Burt and W.E. Thomas. Recent renovation work on one property revealed that old ships' timbers, complete with treenails, had been used for some construction work. This comes as no surprise: with ship breaking and repairing within a stone's throw it is likely that such timbers were used on many Terrace houses.

By the 1930s the Bar Creek had been totally filled in, the old shipyards and small commercial enterprises along Bar Road vanished under rubble. The narrow-gauge railway for the dock excavations extended on the made-up ground as far as the Territorial Army centre. Except for part of Harvey's Yard, a builders' yard, and the hotel and a garage, the site remained undeveloped into the 1980s. What followed has been well-documented in the local press, and comprehensive files lodged in the Cornwall Centre, Redruth. Suffice to say that in December 1987 the town council backed the plans of a development company to build a £20 million harbour village and marina, to be known as Port Pendennis. A few years after the completion of that enterprise, in October 1999 work was begun on a unique structure, built partly over water, partly over what had been Harvey's beach. Three years later, in December 2002, the National Maritime Museum, Cornwall, opened its doors to the public. With access to the impressive record collections held within the county's archive centres, it is hoped that an establishment such as this may provide a focus for research, and promulgate the long and multi-faceted history of maritime Cornwall.

END NOTES

CHAPTER ONE
1 C.R.O., X 1020/1

CHAPTER TWO
1 *Tide Mills*, S.P.A.B., 1955
2 *Exeter Papers in Industrial Archaeology*, 1971
3. C.R.O., K123

CHAPTER THREE
1 Vol.46 No.2, 1960

CHAPTER FOUR
1 *History Detective*, in *Pembrokeshire Life*, Dec. 2006
2 R.C.P.S archive
3 C.R.O., X 263/127
4 *Royal Cornwall Gazette*, Oct. 28 1876

BIBLIOGRAPHY

Acton, Viv, 1993. *Life by the Fal*, Landfall Publications.

Acton, Viv, and Carter, Derek, 1994. *Operation Cornwall, 1940-1944,* Landfall Publications.

Acton, Viv, 1997. *A History of Truro*, Landfall Publications.

Brett, R.L. Ed., 1979. *Barclay Fox's Journal*, Bell and Hyman.

Barnicoat, David, 1998. *Dodman to Black Head*, Packet Publishing.

Bartlett, John, 1996. *Ships of North Cornwall*, Tabb House.

Benney, D.E., 1972. *An Introduction to Cornish Watermills*, Bradford Barton.

Bird, Sheila, 1985. *Bygone Falmouth*, Phillimore.

Bristow, Colin M., 1996. *Cornwall's Geology and Scenery, an Introduction*, Cornish Hillside
    Publications.

Carew, Richard, 1602. *The Survey of Cornwall* (re-issue 2000), Tamar Books.

Davies, Alun, 1995. *The History of the Falmouth Working Boats*, Davies.

Defoe, Daniel, 1724. *A Tour through the Whole Island of Great Britain,* Penguin Books 1971.

Dudszus, A., and Henriot, E., 1986. *Dictionary of Ship Types*, Conway Maritime Press.

Dunston, Bob, 1975. *The Book of Falmouth and Penryn*, Barracuda Books.

Dury, G., 1966. *The Face of the Earth*, Penguin Books.

Eglinton, Edmund, 1982. *Last of the Sailing Coasters*, National Maritime Museum/HMSO.

Gay, Susan E., 1903. *Old Falmouth*, Headley Bros London.

Gilson, Peter, 1992. *The Lower Fal*, Alan Sutton Publishing.

Gilson, Peter, 1994. *The Upper Fal*, Alan Sutton Publishing.

Greenhill, Dr Basil, 1988. *The Merchant Schooners*. Conway Maritime Press.

Greenhill, Dr Basil, Ed., 1993. *Sail's Last Century*, Conway Maritime Press.

Greig, James, Ed., 1926. *Farington Diary, The, Vol 6*, Hutchinson.

Guthrie, A., 1994. *Cornwall in the Age of Steam*, Tabb House.

Halliday, F.E., 1959. *A History of Cornwall*, Gerald Duckworth & Co.

Hussey, David, 2000. *Coastal and River Trade in Pre-Industrial England (Bristol and its Region),* Exeter
    University Press.

Jeffery, H.M., 1886. *The Early Topography of Falmouth*, etc., Journal of the Royal Institution of
    Cornwall, Vo.9, p.147.

Jeffery, H.M., 1886. *The Killigrew Manuscript/The Falmouth Manuscript,* Journal of the Royal
    Institution of Cornwall, Vol.9, p.195.

Kingsford, C.J., 1962. *Prejudice and Promise in 15th Century England*, (Chap.4 on West Country
    piracy), Frank Cass & Co. Ltd.

Kittridge, Alan, 1988. *Passenger Steamers of the River Fal*, Twelveheads Press.

Lake, William, 1867. *Parochial History of Cornwall*, Vol.1, Truro.

Leveridge, B.E., Holder, M.T., Goode, A.J.J., 1990. *Geology of the Country Around Falmouth*, British Geological Survey.

Mathew, David, 1924. 'The Cornish and Welsh Pirates in the Reign of Elizabeth', *English Historical Review*, Vol.39.

McGowan, Alan, 1981. 'Tiller and Whipstaff' *The Ship*, Vol.3, National Maritime Museum.

McGowan, Alan, 1980. 'The Century Before Steam' *The Ship*, Vol.4, National Maritime Museum.

Palmer, June, 1997. *Cornwall, The Canaries and the Atlantic, 1704-19, The Letterbook of Valentine Enys*, University of Exeter.

Parfield, Oliver, 1875. *Pendennis and St Mawes*, W. Lake. Reprint 1984, by Dyllansow Truran.

Pawlyn, Tony, 2003. *The Falmouth Packets, 1689-1851*, Truran Books.

Penaluna, William, 1819. *The Circle – Or Historical Survey of 60 Parishes and Towns in Cornwall*, Penaluna, Helston.

Philbrick, M.E., Redwood, U.M., 1987. *Little Falmouth*, Flushing.

Pollock, John, *Falmouth for Instructions*, Pollock.

Ratcliffe, J., Ed., 1997. *Fal Estuary Historic Audit*, Cornwall Archaeological Unit, Cornwall County Council.

Robinson, Douglas, R.R., 1992. *Bar Pool*, Robinson.

Roddis, Roland, 1951. *Cornish Harbours*, Christopher Johnson.

Sheppard, Peggy and Douglas, 1994. *The Story of Port Navas*, Landfall Publications.

Starkey, David J., 1990. *British Privateering Enterprise in the Eighteenth Century*, University of Exeter Press.

Symons, Alan, 1994. *Falmouth's Wartime Memories*, Arwenack Press.

Tattersfield, Nigel, 1991. *The Forgotton Trade*, Jonathan Cape.

Thomas, Charles, 1985. *Exploration of a Drowned Landscape*, Batsford.

Thomas, Richard R., 1827. *History and Description of the Town of Falmouth*.

Thompson, Hilary, 1994/5. *History of the Parish of Gerrans 1800-1914*, (Part One, *Farms and Farmers*; Part Two, *Mariners and Fishermen*).

Victoria County History of the County of Cornwall, Vol.1, 1906.

Warner, Rev. Richard, 1808. *A Tour Through Cornwall*, London.

Whetter, J.C.A., 1971. *The Rise of the Port of Falmouth, 1600-1800*, paper in *Ports and Shipping in the South West*, Exeter Papers in Economic History, University of Exeter.

Whetter, Dr James, 1981. *The History of Falmouth*, Dyllansow Truran.

Whitley, H.M., 1882. *Dame Killigrew and the Spanish Ship*, Journal of the Royal Institution of Cornwall, Vol.7, XXVII, p.282.

Willan, T.S., 1967. *The English Coasting Trade, 1600-1750*, Manchester University Press.

Williams, J.A., 1961. *The English Channel*, Readers Union/Collins.

Woodcock, Percy, 1925/6. *Quay Punts*, journal Yachting Monthly, Vol.40, No.240. (Other useful articles on quay punts by Woodcock in Yachting Monthly, Vol.1, 1906; Vol.5, 1908; Vol.49, 1930).

Worth, R.N., 1870. *Family of Killigrew*, Journal of the Royal Institution of Cornwall, Vol. 3, XII, P.269.

INDEX

Index of Vessels in the Text Built on the Fal

Other Vessels